Prepared to Preach

D0885795

PREPARED TO PREACH

Pastor Al Martin

Lectures delivered by Pastor A. N. Martin
of Trinity Baptist Church, New Jersey, at the
Banner of Truth Ministers Conference held in
Sydney in August 1979.

Scripture quotations are generally from the
American Standard Version of 1901.

COVENANTER PRESS

First Edition   .   .   .   .   .   .   June 1981

ISBN 0 908189 15 X

Covenanter Press
P. O. Box 48, Strathpine North,
Australia, 4500

CONTENTS

Foreword   7

Chapter 1. The Gifts of the Preacher   9

Chapter 2. The Training of the Preacher   ... 44

Chapter 3. The Call and Commission
                    of the Preacher   ... 71

Chapter 4. The Devotional Life
                    of the Preacher   ... 98

Foreword

In Australia, as in much of the world, this century has witnessed a rapid decline of the true preaching of the Word of God. As the authentic heirs of the Reformation have passed away, there has arisen a generation of unbiblical innovators whose training has been in the schools of heterodoxy and humanism, rather than in the school of Christ. Their rule of faith is the lowest common denominator of ecumenical "easy believe-ism". Their rule of life is pragmatism and expediency, of which the lavish electronic religious concerts and the spectacular city-wide crusade circuses, are but two extreme manifestations.

The preaching of the modern religious superstars and their progeny is experience-centred emotionalism, of a kind which leaves congregations of sinners complacent in their sin and content with a mental assent to a Jesus of whom they know little.

Pastor Albert N. Martin's series of addresses at the 1979 Banner of Truth Conference in Sydney came as a breath of life to us. In the providence of God, he was requested to speak on the theme of the Preacher—his call, commission, gifts, training and devotional life. In no uncertain manner, he wielded the sword of the Spirit against "Lord Expediency, King Pragmatism and Prince Tradition." He set in their place, the King and the Head of the church, the Lord Jesus Christ, by expounding clear biblical principles.

The address on the Preacher's devotional life laid bare the spiritual poverty of many who attended the Conference (including myself, when I heard the tapes later). It has been a labour of love to edit these tapes for publication. In order to preserve something of the power of Pastor Martin's lectures, editorial deletions have been kept to an absolute minimum.

May the Lord of the harvest bless these challenging words of counsel, to the calling and qualifying of labourers for this great task; men prepared to preach the gospel of the grace of God.

June, 1981.

John Amos,
Moderator,
Presbyterian Reformed Church of Australia.

CHAPTER 1.

The Gifts of the Preacher

"Paul, an apostle of Christ Jesus through the will of God, according to the promise of the life which is in Christ Jesus, to Timothy, my beloved child: Grace, mercy, peace, from God the Father and Christ Jesus our Lord. I thank God, whom I serve from my forefathers in a pure conscience, how unceasing is my remembrance of thee in my supplications, night and day longing to see thee, remembering thy tears, that I may be filled with joy; having been reminded of the unfeigned faith that is in thee; which dwelt first in thy grandmother Lois, and thy mother Eunice; and, I am persuaded, in thee also. For which cause I put thee in remembrance that thou stir up the gift of God, which is in thee through the laying on of my hands. For God gave us not a spirit of fearfulness; but of power and love and discipline. Be not ashamed therefore of the testimony of our Lord, nor of me his prisoner: but suffer hardship with the gospel according to the power of God; who saved us, and called us with a holy calling, not according to our works, but according to his own purpose and grace, which was given us in Christ Jesus before times eternal, but hath now been manifested by the appearing of our Saviour Christ Jesus, who abolished death, and brought life and immortality to light through the gospel, whereunto I was appointed a preacher, and an apostle, and a teacher. For which cause I suffer also these things: yet I am not ashamed; for I know him whom I have believed, and I am persuaded that he is able to guard that which I have committed unto him against that day. Hold the pattern of sound words which thou hast heard from me, in faith and love which is in Christ Jesus. That good thing which was committed unto thee guard through the Holy Spirit which dwelleth in us." (2 Timothy 1:1-14)

The subject before us is the gifts of the preacher. Now obviously this is a very vast and expansive subject, and so what I want to do at the outset is to mark out the precise boundaries of our concern.

For our purposes, I am assuming two things:— First, that the gifts to preach and to minister are already present. Secondly, that the gifts have been sufficiently developed so as to warrant their recognition by the people of God and by the church of God, so that the man who possesses those proven gifts is, in the language of the apostle Paul, labouring in the Word and in doctrine.

Our concern will therefore be with the nurture

and the cultivation of those preaching gifts which are already being employed in the work of the ministry. I want to say one other thing by way of introduction.

I do not believe that the Scriptures teach that a Pastor's only task is that of preaching, or that preaching is the only God-given gift that needs cultivation. It is not uncommon for me to spend, in any given week, ten, twelve or sometimes many more hours than that in personal, individual, pastoral shepherding. (I like that term much better than the term counselling, because of the humanistic orientation and connotations that have surrounded the whole concept of counselling.) I certainly do not believe that the Bible teaches that the task of the preacher is done, or is anywhere near complete, when he has preached, or even preached well. So in dealing with this subject 'The gifts of the Preacher' and in particular, the maturing of those gifts, I want it understood that I'm zeroing in only on the public teaching, preaching ministry, because it is so vital and foundational to all else. But this certainly is not the sum and substance of the gifts of the pastor which ought to be present and which, of necessity, need to be cultivated.

First of all we will consider together the necessity for the conscious cultivation of one's preaching gifts; then secondly, the proper motives for the conscious cultivation of one's preaching gifts; and thirdly, some practical directives for the conscious cultivation of one's preaching gifts.

The Necessity

In considering the necessity for the conscious cultivation of one's preaching gifts, I want to bring into focus several very pivotal texts from the pastoral epistles. The first one has already been read in your hearing. Paul was writing to his spiritual son, Timothy, who had been left behind to serve the work of the church there in the area of Ephesus. This was a very strange admonition and command: "For which cause I put thee in remembrance that thou stir up the gift of God, which is in thee, through the laying on of my hands" (2 Tim. 1:6). A more literal translation would be: 'Keep fanning into live flame the charisma of God.' Now without opening up the moot questions regarding the precise nature of Timothy's gift or charisma; or the relationship of that charisma to the laying on of the apostle's hands (and those are indeed moot questions!), one thing is clear, that Timothy is to continue in the conscious cultivation of his God-given gift of ministry. Paul writes to Timothy saying that he, Timothy, is to stir up into living flame this charisma of God. He is not to pray that God will increase the flame of this gift. He is not to pray that others do it. It comes to him as a command; a responsibility that is laid squarely upon Timothy's shoulders. If such a responsibility is true of the more extraordinary gifts that Timothy possesses, and in the light of the more extraordinary way in which those gifts were conferred, how much more is it true in the case of ordinary gifts conferred in an ordinary

12

manner! Do you see the line of reasoning? If any one could slip back and say 'Well my gift came to me in such peculiar circumstances and it is, in a sense, an extraordinary gift; therefore the dimension of the divine enablement; the dimension of the divine initiative in the development of that gift must be supreme, lest in any way I give the impression that this is just an ordinary gift.' If anyone could reason that way, Timothy could; but not after he received Paul's second letter. His conscience was bound by the duty of the conscious cultivation of his God-given preaching gifts.

In chapter two of this same letter we have a similar perspective: "Of these things put them in remembrance, charging them in the sight of the Lord, that they strive not about words, to no profit, to the subverting of them that hear. Give diligence [or properly rendered, do thine utmost] to present thyself approved unto God, a workman that needeth not to be ashamed, handling aright [or cutting a straight course in] the word of truth" (2 Tim.2:14-15). Timothy is charged with this responsibility of constantly doing his utmost, to the end that he may be constituted an unashamed workman. He must so give himself to the cultivation, as well as the exercise of his gifts of ministry, that in the presence of his God there will be no cause of shame when he handles that Word which is the very essence of his ministerial task.

In the first letter of Paul to Timothy, in chapter 4,

13

we find a similar emphasis. Amidst the many duties which Paul had laid upon Timothy with respect to the life and government of the churches, he included: "Neglect not the gift that is in thee, which was given by prophecy, with the laying on of the hands of the presbytery. Be diligent in these things; give thyself wholly to them; that thy progress may be manifest unto all" (1 Tim. 4:14-15).

Here again the apostle says to Timothy that he is never to allow himself to coast; he must never take his hands off the oars and feel that because he has attained to some degree of proficiency; some degree of earned reputation among the people of God, he can simply coast at his present level of ministerial proficiency. No! He is told on the one hand the negative 'neglect not', assuming of course, the contra part in the positive: give constant attention to that gift that was given you by prophecy. Be diligent in these things; so diligent, Timothy, that your own progress, both as a man and a preacher, will be manifest unto all. Timothy, when I come back into that area to talk to people about you, I want everyone to ask: 'Paul, when was the last time that you heard Timothy preach?' My reply will be: 'I heard him preach eight months ago.' 'What did you think of him then?' Then I will answer, 'Oh well, I was pretty proud of my spiritual son; in the right sense of course. He handled the word in a very admirable manner. He cut a straight course in the word of truth.'

Paul exhorts Timothy to make such progress that when that little exchange goes on, people will say: 'Ah Paul, you haven't heard anything yet! There's a richness; there's a zest; there's an unction; there's a precision; there's a bite; there's a grip upon the conscience now, that was never there in Timothy's ministry before.'

Timothy, let your progress be manifest unto all. Now how is this to come? Just with the passing of time? No! Only as Timothy is careful not to neglect the gift that is given to him; as Timothy is careful to be diligent in the cultivation of his God-given gift.

Now surely these texts (and there are others that can be brought into service) establish the duty of the conscious cultivation of one's ministerial gifts. Now we must ask, and have a biblical answer for the very simple question: "Why is this necessary?" If the gift is a charisma of God; if it ultimately finds its origin in the activity of God; in the sovereign will of God; in the efficacious work of the Holy Spirit of God; why must the recipient be so consciously involved in its development; in its maturation; in its improvemen? I know of no text which answers that question, at least in principle, more succinctly and accurately than that pivotal text concerning any questions of this nature, Philippians chapter 2, verse 12:—
"So then, my beloved, even as ye have always obeyed, not as in my presence only, but now much more in my absence, work out your own salvation with fear and trembling; for it is God who worketh in you

both to will and to work, for His good pleasure."

Three Principles

The three great principles in this text that apply so forcefully to the subject in hand are these:

God's working and our working are concurrent realities. "Work out your own salvation with fear and trembling . . ." That is, there is a working out that brings within its orbit the full engagement of all our faculties. There is to be a working out with fear and with trembling; that is, feeling the tremendous weight of the spiritual issues involved. In context of course, Phil. 2:12 refers to the general on-going salvation; but for our purposes we are applying it to the subject of nurturing our gifts. This then, is the first great principle: God's working and the believer's working are concurrent realities.

God's working forms the basis for our working. When the apostle commands the Philippians to work out their own salvation, he gives as the rationale in verse thirteen, "For it is God who worketh in you both to will and to work for His good pleasure." In other words, as Paul exhorts the Philippians to work out their own salvation, he encourages them with the statement that they will never need fear that their working will outstrip God's working. He is constantly at work in His own, to will and to do for His good pleasure.

Our working is the proof and the manifestation of God's working. How does God work? Well look at the text: ". . . it is God who worketh in you both to will

16

and to work . . ." This exposes one of the fatal flaws of the theory of the Christian life which I call the "Funnel Theory". This is the idea of Christ's living His life through you, when you just get so perfectly yielded that every last twitch is out of your little finger, and then His life just flows right through you. Well, that sounds just wonderful for someone who has drooled for such a life for a long, long time. But it violates the perspective of this passage and the entire teaching of the Word of God concerning what we might call the theology of God's working in our working. No! How does God's working come to manifestation? He works in you. In the hidden depths of your redeemed personality, He so works. It is at the level of your choosing and your performing that His work comes to life. He works in you, not to by-pass your willing, nor to negate your working, but He works in you to will and to work for His good pleasure.

Well now, we take that over into the realm of the subject before us. Is a preacher, as long as he has breath, as long as he occupies this sacred office, though he may be experienced and have preached for thirty, forty and fifty years, under a solemn obligation, consciously and constantly to cultivate his preaching gifts? Yes, he is. He is never to feel that he has arrived at a level that will allow him to coast, and the theological reason which lies behind this is the responsibility outlined in such a passage as Philippians chapter 2. God's working and our working are concurrent realities. His working forms the basis for our working. Our working is the proof and the manifestation of His working. Therefore, in preaching, as in every other area of the Christian life, it is the fusion of prayer and pains that results in progress. Not pains without prayer; not prayer without pains; but the fusion of prayer and pains works for progress. This is the coalescing of trust and travail; the welding of reliance and resolve. Here we have the interaction of the natural and of the supernatural; the principles operative in nature and the principles operative in grace.

In the past year, I have had the awesome responsibility of trying to teach young men some principles of preaching. For the first time, I have had to hammer out a relatively expansive and thorough theology of preaching. Well, one of the principles that has come to the fore again and again, is this very principle that God's working and our working are concurrent realities. Some of the great reasons for the paucity of powerful preaching in our day must include the low level of spirituality manifested in prayerlessness and in a careless and cavalier handling of the Word of God, together with sheer unadulterated laziness. But another reason is that there is this subtle fear that there is something carnal about beginning to consciously cultivate our preaching gifts. We're all primed to become nineteenth century pulpiteers and big shots. We're going to obscure the glory of Christ if we develop into good preachers. That's sheer rubbish! The Word of God commands you to stir into living fire the gift of God which is in you. Give yourself wholly to these things, that your progress may be manifested unto all.

Priorities

Now by way of application, let me say that without the conviction that it is our duty consciously and constantly to cultivate our gifts of preaching, we simply will not develop the disciplines and the specific program necessary to increase in our preaching ability. Alexander, in his *Thoughts on Preaching* said something that struck me like a ton of bricks the first time I read it; and each time I re-read it, it hits me again with equal weight. In one of his homiletical paragraphs in which he was writing to young men particularly, he said:

> "To be a good preacher a man must be nothing else. The daily exercises of Demosthenes and Cicero may give us a hint of the devotion which is necessary. The analogy of all other arts and sciences may instruct. There are among us preachers who may be considered good, and in a certain sense great ones, who spend their principal strength during the week upon other pursuits. They write essays, systems and commentaries. It may be observed of them all, that however useful they may be, these are not the men who move, and warm, and melt, and mould the public masses."[1]

You see the contrast? What they write is good. What they say in their public ministries is good. But

---

1. Alexander, J.W. "Thoughts on Preaching" p.10 (B. of T.)

they are not the men who are moving and melting the public masses.

"Indeed, I think, to be a great preacher, a man must lay his account to forego that reputation which comes from erudition and literature. The channel must be narrowed, that the stream may flow in a rapid current, and fall with mighty impression . . . Great is the difference, though little apprehended, between the theological dissertation and the sermon, on the same subject. The crude matter falls heavily upon the popular ear. Only the last exquisite results of mental action are proper for public address."

Then he goes on to enlarge upon that, and he culminates that emphasis with this statement:

"To be powerful in pulpit address the preacher must be full to overflowing of his theme, effected in due measure by every truth he handles, and in full view, during all his preparation and all his discourses, of the minds which he has to reach."[2]

Now, certainly none could accuse Alexander of being an anti-intellectual. He obviously was quite fluent in the biblical languages. He had a background in the classical learning and all of the rest; and yet he was writing to men saying, 'you must determine that if you preach well, you must be willing to do many other things less than to your full capacity.'

Brethren, I trust that these principles from Scripture will convince you that it is your duty as a servant of Christ to give yourself to the conscious cultivation of your preaching gifts.

---

2. Alexander, J.W. "Thoughts on Preaching" p.11 (B. of T.)

Motives

What motives ought to govern us in this cultivation of our preaching gifts? Of all the proper motives for the conscious cultivation of one's preaching gifts, let me suggest three.

First of all and supremely, the approbation of God Himself. Of all the things that Paul could have said to Timothy by which to motivate him to ministerial diligence, notice the motive which he holds high above all others in 2 Timothy 2:15: "Give diligence to present thyself approved unto God, a workman that needeth not to be ashamed, handling aright [or cutting a straight course in] the Word of Truth." In other words, 'Timothy, you are to do your utmost to become an able workman, but in all of that endeavour, Timothy, remember that you are ultimately answerable to the God who has laid his hand upon you, endowed you with a certain measure of gift and has placed you into the work of the ministry; so that in all of this constant cultivation of your gift, may your supreme motive be that of showing yourself approved unto your God Himself. Timothy, when you have done any given sermonic exercise, whatever frown or smile may be found upon the face of whatever person who heard you preach, may it be your constant passion and goal to know that the God who has commissioned you smiles.'

It is obvious that that perspective was very real to the apostle himself, because he could say in 2 Corinthians 2:17, "For we are not as the many,

21

corrupting the word of God: but as of sincerity, but as of God, in the sight of God, speak we in Christ." That awful concept of the minister consciously speaking in the sight of God, is a recurring note in the writing of the apostle. Earlier on in this very chapter, he said "we are a sweet savor of Christ unto God" (v.15). The context is in the work of the ministry.

As we preach, we preach in the presence of God and so, in this matter of the conscious cultivation of our ministerial gifts, particularly our gifts of preaching, our highest motive must be that of the approbation of our God. Brethren, if He has laid His hand upon us, if He has endowed us with certain gifts and capacities, He expects us to trade with those gifts in order to bring a maximum measure of usefulness.

The Faithful Servant

Surely, if the parables of the pounds and the talents teach us anything, they teach us that God expects us to trade well with that which has been entrusted to us. It is not enough that we trade with sufficient energy so as to bring a return that satisfies the rank and file of our people; or even to go so far as to bring a return that may give us some degree of eminence in the midst of our ministerial peers. The great question is this—has any given sermonic exercise so represented the absolute devotion of my mind and heart, that almighty God is pleased when I have delivered my sermon? If He does not smile, of what

22

value are the smiles of our people or of our peers? To his own master a servant shall give account. Everyone of us shall give an account of himself to God.

Saving Men

Then there is a second dimension of motivation that ought constantly to be at work in us, as we seek to perfect our gifts: the salvation and the edification of men. Do you remember that classic chapter dealing with Paul's attitude to the use of his Christian liberty (1 Cor. 9)? Having clearly established the principles, the theology, of liberty in the previous chapter, the apostle goes on to show how that for higher ends, he and his companions often relinquished the exercise of their liberty. They do not relinquish the essence of it. That would be unchristian; but the exercise of it, yes. He says in those well known words of 1 Corinthians 9:22-23: "To them that are without law, as without law, not being without law to God, but under law to Christ, that I might gain them that are without law. To the weak I became weak, that I might gain the weak: I am become all things to all men that I may by all means save some. And I do all things for the gospel's sake, that I may be a joint partaker thereof."

Surely no one who is familiar, even in a cursory way, with the writings of Paul, would attribute to Paul the theology that says the ultimate determination of the salvation of men lies in the hands of a mere mortal. No one writes with greater clarity, or with

23

more repeated emphasis concerning the truth that salvation is all of God and all of grace, than does the apostle. Yet, he is not too fastidious to use this language: 'I am become all things to all men that I may save some.' So convinced was the apostle Paul of the direct relationship between the ordained end and a properly suited means, that he is determined to relinquish liberties left and right, because he is consumed with a passion to be instrumental in the salvation of men.

If you can honestly say with the apostle Paul: "Brethren my heart's desire and supplication to God is for them, that they may be saved" (Rom. 10:1), then you will be able to say with him: "I am become all things that they may be saved."

What Kind of Preaching?

Now how does this affect the matter of preaching? Simply in this way. It is no little thing to seize the interest of the unconverted mind. It is no little thing simply to gain the ears of the unconverted. It is a more difficult thing to storm the conscience and to move the affections; and yet no unconverted man is ever saved until first of all, he gives attention to the Word of God. If you don't have his ears you are never going to pierce his heart. If you don't stab his conscience, you are never going to break his heart! This whole labour of learning how to seize men's attention; how to hook men's ears as it were, so that we may drive barbs into their consciences and that we may, under God, see their hearts crushed—this is

24

a matter that is open for investigation. It is an abuse of the doctrine of divine sovereignty simply to say: 'When God is pleased to give me men's ears, to give me their consciences and to break their hearts, he'll do it in His own time and in His own way.'

When we read the history of preaching, the history of revivals, and the history of the great epochs in the church, with but few exceptions we find common denominators appearing again and again with respect to the questions: 'Who is used of God in conversion work in times of gracious visitation? What kind of preaching hooks the ears, pierces the conscience and breaks the heart?'

There is a kind of preaching that is owned of God in the salvation of men. To the degree that we have a passion to be used in the salvation of men, we will labour at the cultivation of our preaching gifts. This is true also, with respect to the edification of the people of God. Paul could say in that classic statement in 1 Corinthians 14:26, "Let all things be done unto edifying." Remember that the context of these words is the regulating of the exercise of certain gifts that may have been the outworking of an unusual measure of spiritual unction. Yet because they were not intelligible, they could bring no edification. We must study what it is that brings, under the blessing of God, the greatest measure of edification. Our great concern must not be simply to do our job, to receive our remuneration, and to have a modicum of approval from our people! If we long to see our people

25

flourishing in grace, we will be forever studying how to bring the Word to our people in a way that will more and more build them up in Jesus Christ. If we are not simply enamoured with biblical and theological ideas and notions for their own sakes, and mesmerized by the sound of our own voice as those notions take verbal symbols, then we cannot but help to be instruments of grace and blessing to the maximum degree.

If God is using your present level of preaching to grant a trickle of conversions, so that you are seeing, on an average, half a dozen people converted in a year, don't you long that He will make you instrumental in bringing dozens into the kingdom of God? The base line of our theological agreement, in a conference such as this, is that ultimately salvation is the work of God. We believe that. We hold to that, I hope, with all of our hearts. But brethren, we must not ignore the fact that one of the reasons why the Spirit of God may be withholding such blessing, is that He would be putting the premium upon our laziness.

Our Consciences

The third motivation that ought constantly to prod us into conscious cultivation of our gifts, is not only the approbation of God, the salvation and edification of our people, but also the pacification of our own consciences.

In this, the apostle Paul is again our instructor. In the 24th chapter of the book of Acts, Paul, giving one of his many defences, says: "Having hope toward God, which these also themselves look for, that there shall be a resurrection both of the just and of the unjust. Herein [in the light of that great assize; in the light of that day when all men will be made naked] I also exercise myself to have a conscience void of offence toward God and men always" (vs.15-16).

The reality of a future judgment had a tremendous ethical and practical influence upon the apostle. He was engaged in the constant spiritual exercise of maintaining a sensitive, healthy conscience; one that was without offence Godward and manward.

This whole doctrine of conscience needs desperately to be opened up in relation to the work of the ministry and the Christian life. The apostle Paul gives it a central place in the pastoral epistles. In 1 Timothy he says that the first step in the apostasy of those whom he mentions, was to be found in the realm of conscience: "Holding faith and a good conscience; which some having thrust from them made shipwreck concerning the faith; of whom is Hymenaeus and Alexander" (1 Tim. 1:19-20). They did not cast off the faith, that is, the body of orthodox truth, until they began to tolerate a conscience that was uneasy in the presence of truth. Many a preacher starts down the road of apostasy, not by flirting with heresy, but by flirting with an area of ethical and moral controversy with God.

Next to the presence of Christ, there is no greater

27

companion to the minister than that of a good conscience. To have the Lord at your side and a peaceful conscience within your breast—those are the preacher's two greatest companions.

Now, with respect to this matter of being motivated to cultivate constantly and consciously, our preaching gifts. Surely brethren, this matter of a peaceful conscience ought to be no little part of our motivation. Why are you and I relieved of the normal means of providing for our family? Why does the church treasurer hand you a cheque every week, or two weeks, or month? What is the biblical rationale behind your not punching a clock in the shop, in the office, or wherever else it may be? Is it not found in the language of Acts 6 and 1 Timothy 5—that we may give ourselves to prayer and to the ministry of the Word; that we may labour in the Word and in doctrine? Brethren, how may we maintain a good conscience? How can we sit and watch our people give the fruit of their sweat as an act of sacrificial love to God in the midst of a worship service as they bring their tithes and offerings; how can we receive a portion of that sacred offering with a good conscience, if we are not constantly labouring at being better preachers; seeking to labour in the Word and in doctrine with greater and greater efficiency and usefulness?

I lay before you these three very powerful motives for pursuing this duty of conscious and constant cultivation of our ministerial gifts.

28

Practical Directives

Having dealt with the duty of motivations, now thirdly, I would like to lay before you some practical directives for the cultivation of our preaching gifts.

First of all, there must be a constant feeding of the springs of our entire redeemed humanity.

The daily program of the preacher involves such matters as his stewardship as a man before God, his wife, his family and his own physical well-being. I don't want to open up this subject in too much detail at this time; suffice it to say for now, that as surely as it is the whole man who preaches, it is the whole man who must be nurtured, if our preaching is to improve.

I have been very forcefully reminded that the whole man preaches. Trying to preach without my foot has been like trying to preach without a portion of my tongue, or one of my hands. Several times I have had to resist the temptation to rise right out of this chair, because the whole man preaches![3]

Well, if the whole man preaches, the improvement in his preaching will be an improvement that finds its tap-root in the nurture of the whole man. That's why Paul could say in 1 Timothy 4:16: "Take heed [or pay close attention] to thyself." He didn't say just to your mind; to your soul; to your spirit. He says "to thyself." That's where he gives Timothy

---

3. A few days before delivering this address, Pastor Martin sustained a foot injury which necessitated his preaching from a chair. —ed.

a little ad hoc medical prescription later on. He says 'help your belly-ache with a little wine.' Why? Because a man with chronic trouble in his stomach is going to find himself dull and lethargic in his preaching. Paul was simply not shifting from the overall burden of Timothy's maturation, and trying to justify something other than a teetotaller's position, when he said: "use a little wine for thy stomach's sake and thine often infirmities" (1 Tim. 5:23). Paul makes a positive statement when he says, "bodily exercise is profitable for a little" (1 Tim. 4:8). We often take this text to negate physical exercise, but it's a positive statement as it stands. It is only comparative in terms of the next statement: "but godliness is profitable for all things, having promise of the life which now is, and of that which is to come."

Well, why stick all that in the midst of a book laden with practical directives for the preacher, both as to his task and to his own development for that task? Here is the principle: Timothy must learn to feed the springs of his entire redeemed humanity, if he is to grow in ministerial efficiency. There can be no greater mistake than to isolate preaching from the totality of what you are as a redeemed man.

Time and time again preachers, particularly young preachers, sensitive, godly young men, call me and say, "Pastor Martin, I don't know what to do." "Well what's your problem?" "I'm so dull and so dry. My devotions have lost their life. I am listless in prayer. I pray for a few minutes and my mind is drawn off. I have no energy in prayer. There's a dullness; my preaching lacks urgency . . ." And so they go on. Why, you would think for sure that they were just about three degrees away from turning their back on the Lord and leaving the ministry! I usually have two standard questions that I ask them if I know them well. Question number one is, "Do you have any regular period of vigourous physical exercise?" "Oh, no, I don't have time." I say, "Oh, I see." Secondly, I ask: "Do you have any regular planned social time with your wife?" "Well, you see, I'm so busy that . . ." And they go on and on. Then I answer, "All right. Now look, I didn't come offering prescriptions to you. You called me. Right, brother? OK. Now I'm going to give you a little advice. Here's the prescription: You sit down and you work over your daily schedule. And in terms of your own metabolism and your own interest, you work in half an hour at least three to four days a week, of some kind of exercise that will give you total mental diversion; that will cause you to sweat; that will cause your body, that sits at the desk hour after hour, to work up a good sweat. And the whole emotional and physiological effect of that will be amazing. Now I want you to do that for at least three months. And I want you to block out at least a half a day when you spend time with your wife. Put it right in your schedule—I don't care what you do, that's your business! Just spend time with your wife. Now, if your problem hasn't cured itself in three months, just call me back."

Do you know how many times I got the second call? Never! Usually after about a month, he says, "Oh brother, thank you. I must confess the advice seemed very unspiritual when you gave it to me but it works. It's a delight to pray again. It's a delight to get into the Word again!" The problem was that an earnest soul was trying to conduct himself as though he were a disembodied spirit. We are not disembodied spirits! Thank God for the disembodied spirits who minister as ministering servants to the heirs of salvation, but you aren't one of them, and neither am I!

Brethren, if we would increase in preaching efficiency, there must be a constant feeding of the springs of our entire redeemed humanity—the intellectual, the physical, the emotional, the social—all of those things. It is amazing how you can trace out those things right through the epistles. You find them tucked away, at times, in the most unlikely places. I love this one, where Paul says: "God, that comforteth those that are cast down" (2 Cor. 7:6, KJV). Have you ever tried to preach when you are cast down and your spirit feels like lead? Impossible, or well nigh to impossible! God, who comforts those who are cast down, comforted us—How? By reminding us of a great covenant promise? No! By sending an angelic visitation? No! Paul said, "God comforted us by the coming of Titus." One day there was a knock on the door. Titus came through the door and Paul's unmet social needs were met, and his spirit was buoyant again. And a buoyant spirit becomes a contagious spirit in preaching. Isn't it true though? These principles, I say, are there in so many places in the Word of God. So the first practical directive for the cultivation of our preaching gifts is that this constant feeding of the springs of our entire humanity is essential.

Preaching Models

Secondly, there ought to be a constant exposure to good models. I don't mean fashion models.

In great measure preaching is an imitative art. The apostle Paul recognized this. Paul could say to Timothy: "Hold the pattern of sound words which thou hast heard from me" (2 Tim. 1:13). What is that morphē, that form of sound words? What is that apostolic tradition? Paul says, "It is that which you heard from me." He could say to Timothy that he had fully known Paul's manner of life as well as his doctrine and all of these other things: "thou didst follow my teaching, conduct, purpose, faith, long-suffering, love, patience" (2 Tim. 3:10). Then again, in 1 Timothy chapter 4, verse 6, we read, "If thou put the brethren in mind of these things, thou shalt be a good minister of Christ Jesus, nourished in the Words of the faith, and of the good doctrine which thou hast followed until now." Too little has been said about this fact that preaching is, by and large, an imitative art. Because it has been abused by people who become mimics, there is a reaction against this principle.

Biblical Models

Where are the good models to whom we should draw near and from whom we should learn? Let me suggest, first of all, the biblical preachers themselves. We ought to read the prophets and the apostles and our Lord, not only to know what they said for our own edification; not only as the basis of instruction to our people, but also to know how they spoke.

One of the things that has been a constant source of challenge to me is to recognize, not only the tremendous breadth of preaching style in the Word of God, and the legitimacy of every one of those styles, but also the efficiency of those styles. If you have never done this, read through the prophets, not so much to analyse what they were saying in the redemptive, historical setting; what they were saying in terms of its legitimate application to the church today; but simply to analyse the prophets as preachers. Surely, if we are told to take them as examples of suffering in their Christian lives, we are to take them as examples of preachers too. Likewise with the apostles, both in their few and scantily recorded sermons in the book of Acts, and in their epistles—many of which take on the flavour of what we would call pastoral preaching. There ought to be this exposure to good models, especially of course, our Lord Himself—the One who spoke as no man ever spoke; whom the common people heard gladly. Certainly there are elements of our Lord's preaching which would never gain a man the reputation of being elegant in "classical preaching" (or any such terminology). Who cares? If, in following the pattern of our Lord as a preacher, one can have little children sitting upon one's knee, hanging upon the words that come from one's mouth, isn't that reward enough?

Other Models

We ought constantly to expose ourselves to a second category of good models; men whose preaching left a mark in their own generation, and whose sermons or biographies are available to us in this day.

Not every good preacher is known. There will be some great surprises in the Last Day. And not every great preacher, who is known to have made his mark as a preacher, committed anything to writing that is in any way reflective of what he was as a preacher. This is one of the points that J. C. Ryle makes again and again. If you don't have it, I would urge you to get Bishop Ryle's *Evangelical Leaders of the Eighteenth Century*, recently reprinted by the Banner of Truth. I have read that through again with great profit.

When you read excerpts of the few remaining sermons of Whitefield and some of these other men, you may ask, "How in the world would ten thousand people hang upon every word?" Well, there is just so much in the act of preaching that can't be embalmed in printer's ink. In a very real sense, a written discourse is one-dimensional. A tape is two-dimensional. But preaching is about seven-dimensional, because there are so many elements involved in the living preacher communicating to living hearers that cannot be captured. Be that as it may, read the sermons of those who were known as men who knew how to hook the ears of men; who knew how to attack the consciences of men, and who were used of God to break the hearts of men. I refer of course to men such as Spurgeon, Baxter, Elias, Edwards and Owen.

I'm tired of Owen being caricatured as a big elephant, clobbering through the woods. Owen is a preacher. Read his sermon on Psalm 130. That will so bless you, that even though you don't have an ounce of jump in you, at least you'll twitch when you read it. It is some of the most lovely, free, earnest, unfettered gospel preaching to be found anywhere in English literature. We ought to read such preaching and analyse it. What was Owen doing here? Why was he doing it? He was no fool!

Other Examples

A dear friend of mine, when he began to preach, could not be faulted as to his content. But he served up what one could call an amorphous glob of solid biblical stuff. It was sound in terms of its exegesis. There wasn't an ounce of heresy in it, but it was heavy and pedantic and unstructured. So a dear wise man sat down with him and said, "Look, we're going to work on your preaching. I'll tell you what we're going to do. Spurgeon, whatever you want to say for him or against him, knew how to preach. Any man that can carry out a thirty year evangelistic campaign knows something about preaching. So now, what we're going to do is to take a sermon of Spurgeon's each week and read it through. Then we're going to sit down together, and we're going to analyse what it was that Spurgeon was doing, and that you're not doing." So they did this. The first thing he said was that Spurgeon had heads. You knew where he was, where he was going; and when he got there, you knew how he got there and where he had been. He said, "Now you've got no heads in your sermon. You don't know where you are, where you're going and if you're ever going to get there. So we're going to start structuring the sermons. What else did Spurgeon do? Well he wasn't beneath speaking down to the children. He wasn't beneath using what some would say were almost silly, earthy illustrations, analogies and metaphors. You start doing that." This dear wise man, working with this preacher unto God, by bringing him close to a good model, was instrumental in helping him to become an able preacher. I would walk twenty miles any day of the week to hear him preach, just from the standpoint of hearing good preaching where the Word of God is served up in such a way that it fastens upon the ear.

Read Bishop Ryle as an example—not so much as an exegetical preacher but, in terms of structure, of the ability to go to the conscience; the ability to take great themes and make them bite and stick. Read McCheyne's sermons. There are any number available to us brethren. Read them with this end in view, that we want to learn what it is to develop that ability to seize the ears and to move the hearts. Then of course, hear any men of our own day who are speaking well and with authority, even though they may not be Reformed. Listen to men who are preaching and are gaining and keeping the attention of men. Preaching is an imitative art. I urge you to expose yourself to good models.

Competent Critics

The third suggestion I would make is this. Not only the constant feeding of the springs of your redeemed humanity, constant exposure to good models, but now this suggestion is going to separate the men from the boys—there must be the constant input of competent critics. Here the book of Proverbs ought to be our companion: In the multitude of counsellors there is safety. Reproofs of instruction are a way of life.

God has some pretty strong things to say about the man who is so bristling with his own sense of self importance that he can't be reproved. God describes him with a very simple word. He calls him a fool. I'm amazed how many ministerial fools there are who do not welcome constructive criticism that would help make them better preachers. Seek to surround yourself with this input at various levels.

For instance: as to the theological content of

your preaching, mark out the most discerning men in your congregation. Whether they are office bearers or not, ask them: "If, in my week by week preaching, you notice theological imprecision; where I don't quite have the pieces put together as I ought; where what I say in the first ten minutes of the sermon, I undo in the last ten minutes; please come to me. I want to be precise." Popular preaching that is theologically precise is not only a beautiful thing, but also it carries tremendous weight in establishing a stable congregation of God's people, who will have discernment and be able to detect error.

Then, find those who are most helpful in mechanical details. You may have an able layman who is not much of a theologian, and will never be much of a theologian, but is a good grammarian. One of our elders is both a good theologian and a good grammarian. Whenever there is a grammatical mistake which is obviously part of a developing pattern, there'll be a lovely little note in the mail that begins "Dear Brother". Then he just lays it out very nicely for me. I welcome that. I urge him to do it. Some of you will remember the dear old soul who would hand Spurgeon a little slip of paper whenever he had made a verbal slip.

Another area, brethren, is one that I would call our 'Pastoral Manner'. In other words, there are dear saints who sense when you are preaching with those mingled elements of pathos, pastoral love, tenderness and intimacy. They also sense when other elements enter, such as a scolding that makes their own spirits chill. They love you. They love your doctrine; but they also love the exuding of a shepherd's spirit, and they are very discerning when something else is coming through. Learn who those people are, and surround yourself with their criticism. Likewise, seek those old saints that are wise in their experience. I call them my 'experimental critics'. Those who have been disciplined in the fire, and those who have been purified by the constant dealings of God. Then of course seek, wherever possible, to have your fellow elders a constant sounding-board. I feel there are few compliments that are higher for a minister than to be not constantly, but frequently approached with kind, gracious, constructive criticism. It's a wonderful compliment, because if someone comes to you, and in a kind and gracious way, gives a constructive criticism, they are saying:

(a) I believe you to be a Christian man who wants to improve.

(b) I believe you are a humble man who is not too proud to listen to criticism.

(c) I believe you are a man who, with all your heart, wants to please your Lord, and if you can improve, you are going to please him more.

That's a lovely compliment. And yet brethren, I am amazed. I do not speak out of ignorance, or out of a vacuum, but out of the context of dozens and dozens of minister's conferences over the years and hundreds of personal interviews. Many a minister has insulated himself from this kind of criticism and he wants it that way. That is nothing but hellish pride! "I'm the Reverend!" Who cares that you're the Reverend, if you are not edifying your people because of a pompous aloofness; because of an academic stiffness; because of a pedantic manner. It's like six elephants walking through quicksand to get from your first point to your last point and it's an exercise in Spartan-like diligence to stay awake through one of your sermons. It's high time you had a few people who come and tell you so. (I don't know what I would say to you if I was standing, so you be thankful I'm sitting.)

Let me say this last word. It is so necessary. If we are to improve in our preaching gifts, there ought to be constant interaction with the masters of the subject of preaching. 1 Corinthians 12 indicates that there is a diversity, not only of gifts, but of administration; and in the history of the church, God has given special competence to some men, not only in the act of preaching, but in the ability to analyse the activity of preaching. They are God's gifts to us. Don't listen to the unproven theorists. Few things get me more angry than to see a book on preaching by a man who has never preached his way out of a paper bag. Such a man has never, under God, preached into existence a solid church, a thriving church; and yet he has the temerity to tell the world how to preach. I wouldn't give you a nickel for the dust-jacket on his book!

Study men who were known to be preachers; men

whom God let live long enough to sit back and analyse the holy art of preaching. You and I ought to be interacting with them continually. Who am I referring to? Men such as Spurgeon, whose *Lectures to My Students* you ought to be reading constantly. I'm so thrilled that Dabney's *Sacred Rhetoric* is coming out in a new garb, called *R. L. Dabney on Preaching.* Brethren, I cannot say enough about that book. It will help you immensely in the matter of your preaching. There is another one that I hope we can get reprinted. A friend of mine just bought it for $26.50. It is Gardner Spring's book *Power in the Pulpit.* Then I will always stand by Bridges' *The Christian Ministry* and Alexander's *Thoughts on Preaching.* Don't despise the jumbled format of Alexander's book. Of course, there's Broadus' *On the Preparation and Delivery of Sermons,* Shedd's *Homiletics and Pastoral Theology* and Lloyd-Jones' *Preaching and Preachers.* Then there is James Stewart's excellent little book, *Heralds of God.* Some of the Yale lectures on preaching are useful. I am amazed at how few preachers are constantly interacting with the masters of the preaching art. It is the only profession as such, where I know that this isn't done! Recently, a surgeon whom I met in another country last year, was in the States. He spent some time with us. He came all the way over to New York City and was going to many countries in the world to do one thing. He has, by personal correspondence, found all the masters in the surgical fields in which he practises. He has written requesting that he might spend a week with them, going from the operating theatre to the bedside, so as to have this close, intimate interaction with the masters of his field. If this principle applies in the saving of men's bodies, how much more should it apply in the saving of men's souls.

Well brethren, I trust these things will prove to be of help and profit to us as we seek to cultivate and stir into flame, the gift of God that is in us. Amen.

CHAPTER 2.

The Training
of the Preacher

As far as I am concerned this is one of the most profoundly important questions that face the church of Jesus Christ at this critical time in her life and ministry. This subject *The Training of the Preacher* is both vast and weighty. In addressing myself to this subject I wish to set forth five broad biblical principles which I would assert should regulate all of our thinking and all of our endeavours in this area. However, in order to relieve these principles of the pressure of unnecessary prejudice or of misunderstanding, I want to underscore on the threshold of our study, three fundamental presuppositions which undergird and condition all that I say.

Brethren, I do believe these matters are vital. If we are to think correctly on anything we must first of all analyse the question: 'from what perspective are we thinking?'

The Authority and Sufficiency of Scripture

The first presupposition which conditions everything that I will say regarding the subject of the training of the preacher is the authority and sufficiency of Scripture with respect to the issue of ministerial training. Too long have King Pragmatism, Lord Expediency and Prince Tradition governed the church in this very sensitive area.

Our Protestant and evangelical heritage is comprehensively and beautifully stated in chapter one of the Westminster Confession of Faith, the chapter on Scripture. We read in paragraph six these very vital words:

> "The whole council of God concerning all things necessary for His own glory, man's salvation, faith and life, is either expressly set down in Scripture, or by good and necessary consequence may be deduced from Scripture: unto which nothing at any time is to be added, whether by new revelations of the Spirit or traditions of men."

Then of course, going on to state the place of the inward illuminating work of the Spirit, the Confession says: "and there are some circumstances concerning the worship of God, and the government of the Church" (and we might say, of ministerial training), "common to human actions and societies, which are to be ordered by the light of nature, and Christian prudence, according to the general rules of the Word, which are always to be observed." Everything necessary for man's faith and life is either expressly set down in Scripture, or by just and necessary

45

inference may be deduced from Scripture.

Now both the Scriptures and church history reveal that no factor is more influential in determining the condition of the churches than the state of the church's ordained ministry. I believe all of us would agree to that statement. Whether we view the condition of the Old Testament Church or the New Testament Church, or whether we review the history of the church subsequent to the closing of the Canon, nothing is more influential in determining the state of the churches than the state of its official ministry.

Furthermore it is clear that no factor is more determinative in conditioning the state of the ministry than is the formal training to which men are subjected in their most formative years. So you see my line of reasoning. The state of the Church is conditioned primarily and fundamentally by the condition of its stated ministry. The condition of the stated ministry is most primarily conditioned by the formative influences which impinge upon that ministry in the most supple, pliable, formative years.

To assume or to act as though Scripture were silent, or not worthy to be considered on this vital issue, is to impugn the wisdom or to insult the authority of Jesus Christ the Head of the Church, who ever lives, not only to intercede for His church, but to nourish and to cherish His church unto its intended perfection. Therefore my fundamental pre-supposition in the formation of this study, is that the Bible does contain a theology of ministerial training, and that it is our responsibility to discover that theology, and having discovered it, begin to implement it at any cost. We must do this even at the cost of taking the Sword of Truth and Radical Reformation and driving it right into the innards of Lord Expediency, King Pragmatism and Prince Tradition, and leaving them to lie wallowing in their blood, brethren, if that is what obedience to the Word of God requires.

Viable Biblical Models

The second fundamental presupposition is this, that there is flexibility and variety in viable biblical models of ministerial training. In other words, once we come to grips with the principles that grow out of exegesis and begin to consider how those principles will be 'fleshed out' in any given specific structure, it is my presupposition (and I believe it can be demonstrated Scripturally) that there is both flexibility and variety in viable biblical models.

One of the great hallmarks of religious life under the New Covenant is its adaptability to the breadth of the application and extension of religious life within this Covenant. The New Covenant operates among all the nations. That means that there must be flexibility and adaptability, because among all the nations one does not have the structured sociological, cultural, educational and other factors that could be found in the Theocracy. Because of this breadth of cultural differences and educational and technological factors, one cannot help but expect

47

to find that in the outworking of biblical principles into models of theological education, there will be variety and flexibility. But beneath that variety and flexibility there ought to be a bottom line, a common denominator of unchanging biblical principles. I believe this can be established simply by a study of the patterns of ministerial training in the Old and the New Testaments. For instance, consider the whole subject of the sons of the prophets. I have been preaching through the life of Elisha in recent months on Lord's Day evenings. I have been drawn back again and again to this whole subject of the sons of the prophets and the unique place which they held in that dark period of Israel's history; and there are some marvellous principles of ministerial training in that section of holy Scripture.

When we turn to the New Testament, the pattern by which the apostle trained such men as Mark, Timothy, Titus and others shows flexibility and variety. But underneath it there are some common denominators. I may, in illustrating some of the biblical principles, of necessity, draw from the concrete situation of our own Ministerial Academy. But it would grieve me if anyone were to assume that I am absolutising in the application of the principle. We may take a principle and express it in one possible viable model. But please do not think that one expression of the principle in a specific viable model is an absolutising of that principle, as to preclude all other models.

The Minister:
Theological Scholar, Preacher and Shepherd of Souls

There is a third presupposition with which I am working, and that is the inseparability of the minister as a theological scholar and as an able preacher and shepherd of souls. I am not addressing myself to the moot question as to whether or not there should exist graduate schools for specific theological studies (perhaps that could be a topic for discussion). I am addressing myself to the question: how are men to be trained for the task of labouring in the Word and in doctrine? How are they to be equipped for the task of shepherding the flock of God? How are they to be influenced so as to fulfil the directives of such passages as Acts chapter 20, 1 Peter chapter 5 and other parallel passages in the New Testament?

Now since the major (not the exclusive) responsibility of this office is bound up in such language as "able to exhort in sound doctrine and to convict the gainsayers", or "feed the flock of God which is among you, taking the oversight not of constraint", it is obvious that the pastor, to fulfil these functions, must in the truest sense be a theological scholar. He must have the tools necessary to accurately exegete the Word of God. He must have so mastered those parabiblical disciplines as to condition his exegesis, his application, and the other dimensions of his ministerial labours.

But since the great end for which the truth of God was given was the salvation and edification of the church, I am assuming that the acquisition of his scholarly attainments will be conditional upon his ability to do the work of a pastor. Let me illustrate. A man in medical school must subject himself to a tremendous amount of technical knowledge, starting with some of the elementary matters of anatomy in which he must learn every muscle, every bone, every kind of tissue in the human body, every organ and its functions, and the inter-relationship between the organs and their various functions. Among the medical students I have talked to, hardly a one of them does not feel many times, in the course of his preparation, 'what in the world is the use of all of this?'

There is a great end in view. All of this technical knowledge, all of the acquisition of these technical terms and insights have as their ultimate goal the the practice of medicine. So that when you show up at the physician's office and you say to him, 'Doc, I've got a funny kind of ache somewhere over here in the right side a little bit above, or a little bit below this part of me; can you find out what's wrong with me?'—Well, it is at that point that you see that the full breadth of the physician's technical training finds its moment of truth.

You do not want a physician who simply has a nice manner, a pleasing personality, gentle hands and a soothing voice. You want to know that all of his tenderness and gentleness and sensitivity has behind it a tremendous breadth and depth of technical knowledge. But the end of all of that knowledge is that of being a competent physician.

In the same way I am assuming in presupposition number three in this lecture that there is of necessity, an inseparability between the minister as a theological scholar and as an able preacher and shepherd of souls. Too long these things have been viewed as if being one precluded being the other. Too long it has been assumed, and often even stated, that the man who has the keen mind, a theological ear, motivation to read deeply in theology and to understand distinctions that the average layman does not understand (and couldn't care less about) should become the professional theologian. Let him take the chair of systematics at the local college!

No, no, my brethren! A man must be a true theological scholar in order to be an accurate and able preacher and shepherd of souls.

Now with those three fundamental presuppositions beneath us and conditioning all that follows, think with me now as I attempt to set before you five biblical principles concerning the whole subject of the training of the minister.

Principle No. 1

None should be admitted to a framework of special theological training but men of proven Christian character and proven ministerial gifts. (My terminology is deliberately general so as to include within this framework, training in a college, Bible school, seminary or a tutorial relationship with a pastor). The case for this principle appears to me to be clearly established by 2 Timothy 2:2.

Among the many duties that the Apostle Paul laid upon Timothy in the oversight of the churches in Ephesus and in that area round about, was included this: "Thou therefore, my child, be strengthened in the grace that is in Christ Jesus. And the things which thou hast heard from me among many witnesses, the same commit thou to faithful men, who shall be able to teach others also" (2 Tim. 2:1-2). Timothy had received the form of sound words from the apostle. Earlier in this chapter he had been charged to hold to that pattern (*morphē*), that form of sound words, that apostolic tradition; the body of revealed truth. But you see, Paul was not only concerned that Timothy, as his representative, hold to and expound that body of apostolic tradition, but also he was concerned for the perpetuity of the teaching office. So he laid upon Timothy the responsibility to see to it that other men, competent to teach others, were properly trained in that body of apostolic tradition.

Now notice how careful he was in setting out the standard for this activity: "Timothy the things you have heard from me, the same commit . . ." In other words (as we shall see later) originality is not to be the hallmark of the theological instructor. He is to be content to say, "I have a deposit of truth received from another. I have no new little wrinkle to inject", and thereby prove his worth by being clever. I am sick and tired of this mentality in our theological colleges; as though the only justification for the professional theologian is novelty! Usually when a man writes his doctoral thesis he becomes so myopic that he cannot see anything in balance until he is sixty years of age. Not always, but generally. He has lived with that which justifies his Ph.D. for so long that he sees the whole Bible through the glasses of his particular area of discipline.

I remember spending a whole summer one time with a dear young brother who was doing his doctoral thesis on the Pauline concept of solidarity. Here we were, working with little children in a child evangelism camp, in which I was the evangelist and he was one of the workers and counsellors. You wouldn't believe it; everything from a child's belly-ache to the most profound problem, he approached from this view-point: "Ah, if only we could come to grips with the Pauline concept of solidarity, we could resolve that problem!" The Pauline concept of solidarity was the issue that would unlock and open up every problem!

Notice the emphasis: "Timothy . . . the things that thou hast heard . . . commit", i.e. "the body of truth you are to pass on." But to whom is Timothy to pass it on? The qualifications are clear: "the same commit thou to faithful *(pistois)* men, who shall be able to teach others also." Timothy is to find, first of all, men of proven Christian character. Many of you know that the word *pistois* can refer either to believing men or to that which is the fruit in character of faith, and hence in some contexts it is translated

53

'trustworthy'. I believe that in this context, it is clearly the latter use of the word. Paul was saying, "Timothy, the things you have received from me commit to trustworthy men, men of proven character."

Notice that he does not say 'commit these things to every keen-minded, theologically-interested young man who happens to apply for this trust of apostolic deposit.' He does not say 'take under your wing every starry-eyed aspirant who has visions of being Whitefield incarnate.' No, no! He was saying, in effect, "Timothy, commit these things to trustworthy men; men whose life and character, amidst all of the manifold pressures of the church, have demonstrated that they are indeed worthy of this trust."

Secondly, he says "who shall be able to teach *(hikanos)*", pointing to being worthy or fit to teach; thereby suggesting some manifestation of God-given ability to perform the task. It is not enough that there be proven eminence in grace. There must be some demonstrative or demonstrated ability to teach. Much can be done to perfect a man's gifts to teach and to preach the Word of God. But little can be done to give what is not there. Spurgeon, who again and again observed this in his own college, said that no man can give to another man the ability of public utterance. Either God gives it to him or God withholds it. The manner in which it is given is complex. Some of it has to do with certain things that were worked into a man's personality, into his physiology, when he was knit together in his mother's womb. The formative influences of education, the home, temperament, also contribute. Granting all of those variables, Timothy was not to commit this deposit merely to trustworthy men, but to men who would be worthy or fit to teach others also, for no amount of grace or sincerity will substitute for the ability to speak.

There is a very interesting article on the whole subject of the call to the ministry in volume 4 of Thornwell's works (for which many of us owe a great debt again to the Banner). Thornwell was so insistent on this point because he saw this issue being kicked back and forth in his day. The church says "well, we'll trust the seminary to see if they have ability to teach", and the seminary says "well, we'll trust the church", and so, like ping pong, they just kept batting it back and forth. This is what Thornwell said on this issue:

> "It ought not to be a matter of course that a young man who has completed the curriculum of studies prescribed in the Seminary is licensed by the Presbytery; his call and gifts should be as thoroughly scrutinized as if they had undergone no scrutiny before. To take the endorsement of the Theological Professors as sufficient proof of his fitness for the office is a criminal neglect of its own duties."[1]

There must be scrutiny. Are they able to teach? If we are to have a biblically based theology of ministerial training, then none should be admitted to a framework of special theological training but men of

---

1. Thornwell, James Henley. "Collected Writings" Vol.4, p.31
   (Banner of Truth)

proven Christian character and proven ministerial gifts. If we take 2 Tim. 2:2 seriously, I can see no other conclusion.

Now, do you see why this would be radical? It would mean that some of you would bring upon yourselves the frown of that godly man or woman who raised their son for the church, and gave him to God to be a minister while he was yet in his mother's womb. But God, who knit him together in his mother's womb, may not have knit him together in such a way as to endow him with the mental and mechanical gifts necessary for the ministry. I cannot imagine what it must be like to cower before the well-meaning pious intentions of godly people, when whole congregations will have to suffer from our indulgence. You would then have to listen to such a man week after week, and say with Cain, "my punishment is more than I can bear!"

Principle No. 2

None should be permitted to continue in a course of special theological training who do not manifest a growing conformity to the Biblical standard for an elder.

If we were to ask a young man of some proven Christian character and proven ministerial gift in a given theological college or framework of specialised training, "Young man, why are you here, doing what you are doing?" I hope his answer would be, "I am here because I aspire to the work and to the office of an elder. With all my heart I long to become an undershepherd under the great shepherd and serve my Lord and His church." Well, if that is so, immediately the standard of 1 Timothy 3 no longer becomes theoretical nor optional, because the text says, "Faithful is the saying, if a man seeketh the office of a bishop he desireth a good work." You know something of the strength of these two key words. One is the word from which we get our word lust, the other means 'to stretch out after'. "If any man seeketh the office of a bishop, he desireth a good work", and so the young man is to be encouraged if he has proven gifts and character.

The Apostle says, "the bishop therefore . . ." (then we have that particle of necessity *dei*) "**must** of necessity be . . ." Then the Apostle gives us a list of characteristics which is neither wooden nor inflexible nor all-inclusive. If that were so, then there would be no difference between the list here and that in Titus. What he has given us is a general description of balanced, matured Christian character and developed competence in the gift of teaching and preaching. But the point for our study is this: "The Bishop therefore **must** be . . ." The things listed there are not manifested like the light that comes from the stroke of lightning, but these graces of character are like the sun that begins to shed its rays as it comes up over the horizon and grows stronger and stronger with each passing moment and hour until, at its zenith, it stands above us in the full blaze and heat of its own glory.

If a young man is aspiring to this office, then God says he must be such a man as is described in this passage. Therefore, to encourage a man to pursue formal training for that office while he is not concurrently manifesting increasing conformity to the prerequisites for that office, is to encourage him in a course of disobedience and self-deception. Dabney, speaking to this very issue in his excellent essay on a call to the ministry, says:

> "This leads us to add another important class of texts by which the Holy Spirit will inform the judgment, both of the candidate and his brethren, as to his call. It is that class in which God defines the qualifications of a minister of the Gospel.
>
> "Let every reader consult, as the fullest specimens, 1 Timothy 3:1-7, Titus 1:6-9. The inquirer is to study these passages, seeking the light of God's Spirit to purge his mind from all clouds of vanity, self-love, prejudice, in order to see whether he has or can possibly acquire the qualifications here set down. And his brethren, under the influence of the same Spirit must candidly decide by the same standard whether they shall call him to preach or not."[2]

Here brethren, I confess to a sense of bafflement and brokenness of heart. It has been my privilege to minister on more than one occasion, in what are considered the outstanding Reformed and evangelical seminaries in our own country, and I don't know of one of them that takes these passages seriously, in its oversight of the young men under their care. Let

---

2. Dabney, R.L. "Discussions: Evangelical and Theological" Vol.2, p.29 (Banner of Truth)

a man be admitted by the recommendation of his session, his elders or his deacons (whatever the church government is). Let him begin to manifest sufficient competence to pass the course of instruction given; but whether or not he manifests growing conformity to the standard of 1 Timothy 3 and Titus 1 is not a matter of concern at all! He will still get his 'sheepskin' or whatever degree is offered, be recommended back to presbytery or to the denomination, and then he will be a candidate for the ministry. Brethren, this is highhanded indifference, if not a spirit of anarchy, against the standard of King Jesus in His Holy Word!

"The Bishop therefore **must** be . . ." Therefore, you see that the training situation must be so structured as to make observation of character and gift both extensive and influential. The mere attendance of classes and the handing in of exams is not enough, and something must be done. Here I call for radical revolution, not radical implementation. It may take years, but let us get our biblical vision and hitch, as it were, our perspective to the star of biblical standards. It may take us ten to twenty years to get there. But far better this, than to accept the status quo. Someone came to a black preacher and said, "Preacher, I hears all the time 'bout the status quo. What's the status quo?" And he said "that's the mess we's in, that's the mess we's in!" Well, that's the mess we's in, and brethren, this will cost.

I want to introduce a true story. When we

59

hammered out this principle in our prospectus for our own Ministerial Academy which began two years ago, we made it very plain that at the end of each year, a man's character as well as his gift would come under the close scrutiny not only of his instructors the elders, but of his peers. They would be asked "What kind of influence has this man had upon you?" Also there was an individual interview with each of the students evaluating his own peers. Then our moment of truth came when we had to call a man in and sit him down and say to him, 'Sir you are not welcome to return to the Academy next year. Your marks are excellent, your academic ability unquestionable, but the unanimous consent of your fellow students, the consent of your instructors and the elders is that in certain areas (and we outlined them again) you are deficient.' Each of these areas was critical to the work of the ministry, according to the standards of 1 Timothy 3. We said "Were we to retain you in the Academy, we would be saying, 'you are a bonafide candidate for the office of an elder.' Eight months later he came into my study and said, 'Pastor Martin, I want you to convey a message to the elders and to the instructors, and the message is this: I thank you for having the moral courage to deal with me according to the Word of God. It has become the basis now of my understanding, that the will of God for me is not the work of the ministry.' He then went on to say how God has opened a new dimension of usefulness and service for him.

Here was the principle: None should be permitted to continue in a course of special theological training who do not increasingly manifest a conformity to the biblical standard for the ministry. Do you know what encouraged us? We were not doing anything new. In the good providence of God, I came across the original Charter of Princeton Seminary. The belief of its originators was that religion without learning or learning without religion in the ministers of the Gospel must ultimately prove injurious to the church. The General Assembly which approved the measures authorising the establishment of the Seminary, sought to maintain the proper balance by including amongst its eight resolutions, one which dealt with the necessity of the fusion of learning and piety in every student. Then, in the out-working of that resolution this section was then drafted:

> "It ought to be considered as an object of primary importance by every student in the seminary to be careful and vigilant not to lose that inward sense of the power of Godliness which he may have attained, but on the contrary to grow continually in the spirit of enlightened devotion and fervent piety, deeply impressed with the recollection that without this, all his other acquisitions will be comparatively of little worth, either to himself or to the church of which he is to be a member."

Then they outlined what they meant. The Lord's Day was to be given to self-examination, including the student's scrutiny of his own heart, his progress in grace and his progress over his own besetting sins.

61

The professors were to watch carefully the students in this area. The Charter continued:

> "If any student shall exhibit in his general deportment a levity or indifference in regard to practical religion, though it do not amount to any overt act of irreligion or immorality, it shall be the duty of the professor who may observe it, to admonish him tenderly and faithfully in private, and endeavour to engage him to a more holy life and a more exemplary deportment. If a student after due admonition, persist in a system of conduct not exemplary in religion, he shall be dismissed from the seminary."

Think of it, not scandalous sin such as chasing women until three in the morning! Simply sleeping in on the Lord's Day and not being found in a house of worship. Spending the Lord's Day afternoon watching the football and soccer matches instead of searching his own heart! In our evangelical and Reformed seminaries, students do this, Lord's Day after Lord's Day, and no rebukes come, no admonition comes, and yet they say they are going out to lead the people of God. Brethren this is a tragic situation and I trust it does not happen here. But human nature being what it is, I would be greatly surprised if it does not happen to some degree.

Principle No. 3

The predominant moulding influence in the framework of special theological training must be exerted by men of proven competence and eminence in the work of the ministry.

When we turn to the Scriptures with the question, "what kind of men were marked out by God to mould and train others for spiritual leadership?", the answer is clear, consistent, and overwhelming. To put it another way, in Scripture we find instances where God laid his hand upon a man, or a group of men, to train and influence other men for the work of the ministry. What kind of men did he appoint for that task?

Gardner Spring, addressing himself to this issue in his book *Power in the Pulpit* says:

"Our second reply to the question is, let the teachers of those who are being educated for the ministry be men of no inconsiderable experience in the pastoral office. In the early organisation of theological seminaries the professors were of this character. They came with the experience of settled pastors; not with clear heads only, but with warm hearts, and from the warm bosom of churches which they loved. Their more early pupils were the flower of the churches. They preached as though they understood and felt the Gospel, and though not a few of them have been called to their rest, their names will long be embalmed in the memory of good men. We say this is a wise arrangement, for there is no prima facie testimony to the personal qualification of a teacher of young men who are pursuing their studies with a view to the ministry, as that which is furnished by having usefully and acceptably sustained the responsibilities of the pastoral office. There is no such test of his intellectual and spiritual qualifications, of his tact as a teacher, of his habits and industry, and his capacity and willingness to endure hardness as a good soldier of Christ. If the Deacons must first be proved (1 Timothy 3), much more the ministers, and if ministers, much more the instructors of ministers.

63

The more deliberately and impartially the subject is considered, the more it will be found to be one of the most absurd things in the world to invest a man with the office of a teacher of the sons of the prophets who is himself no prophet."

Spring calls it absurd. He continues:

"It requires but an ingenuous and impartial view of this question in order to produce the strong conviction that the rule ought rarely, if ever, to be dispensed with, not even in favour of those departments which, from their own nature, are most purely scholastic, and for the competent occupancy of which, young men must be specially trained."

Of course he was speaking of such things as the languages and some of the more technical disciplines. Then he goes on to say:

"Theological science, as a science, has no peculiarity. It is in this respect like every other science. No man understands it until he has practiced it."

Then he goes on to enlarge upon this fact, that men who are theologians out of the womb of a living ministry impart a flavour, an unction, a penetration, an insight to their theologising in the classroom that the mere professional can never do. Again, I do not know what it's like here in Australia, but often in the USA, a young man comes right out of High School; right out of Secondary School. He is converted. He has an appetite for theology so he does, perhaps, an undergraduate degree majoring in philosophy or history to give him a broad liberal arts background. Then he goes on and he does a B.D. or master's degree in divinity. If he shows more precociousness in theology, he gets a full grant to do his Ph.D. So he goes off to Amsterdam or to Edinburgh or to Aberdeen and he gets his Ph.D. And coming back at age 30, having done nothing but sit in classrooms for 12 years, he has the sons of the prophets sitting before him and he has to mould them into able ministers of the New Covenant!

I know of no other field in which this would be tolerated. Who are the chief resident surgeons in our hospitals, teaching young doctors how to cut open a man's thoracic cavity and go in and take out a cancerous lung? Who? Not the man who's been studying books on internal surgery for 12 years! They are the men who have been in the operating theatre and have laid open chest after chest after chest, and have healthy patients after healthy patients, as monuments of their competence. Who teaches young aspiring professional rugby league players how to play? The man who has been out there and had his own head banged up in the scrum. You don't take the man who has been at the library studying all about it for 10 years!

Brethren it is ridiculous! Who become the golf professionals and instruct people as to how to stroke a ball? Men who themselves have won a tournament here or there, stroking a ball. But when it comes to the ministry we have this strange notion that all that needs to be learned can be learned from books in the academic detachment of a seminary. I say it is time some of us reared back on our hind legs and said, "enough!"

Our churches are drying up. Why? Well there are many reasons, but not the least is that these are men who have caught no fire. They have never had their systematic theology crackling with the fire of an impassioned pastoral heart. They are not learning it from men who have seen that proper Christology becomes as it were, the very open door to the deepest devotion, to the warm and holy and passionate attachment to the Son of God. Forgive me brethren, if I become earnest on this point, because I feel it so deeply. The tragic results of the failure to grasp this principle are with us to this very hour.

Spring throws out a challenge which I have never seen answered. I actually had the temerity to throw this challenge right in the face of a whole faculty who had one man, I think, in the whole faculty who had had two years' pastoral experience. All the rest had none at all. Spring said,

> "We have sought to ascertain that the Scriptures anywhere contemplate a class of theological teachers who have not themselves been the acknowledged and honoured teachers of the people. Unless we have overlooked some important fact, the history of the Jewish and Christian Church speaks the same language from the days of Samuel to the days of Paul, and it is uniformly in favour of the views here expressed."

It is easy to say *sola scriptura,* but when *sola scriptura* makes an impingement on the traditions of theological training it is quite another issue.

Principle No. 4

The conscious concentrated and integrating factor

of the entire specialised theological training should be the development of able preachers and competent shepherds of souls.

The duties and functions as given in the pivotal passages such as Acts 20, 1 Peter 5, and in particular the pastoral epistles, must be examined, expounded and integrated into the whole overall training framework. Here again, the proven guides are so essential. If we are to develop able preachers and competent shepherds of souls, as well as to the writings of such men. I question the wisdom of any system of theological training which makes men more acquainted with Bultmann and the vacillating Berkhouwer, than with John Owen and with William Cunningham. I don't understand it! Why plow through Berkhouwer today, when he may say something different tomorrow, the worth of which may all be shown in its true light fifty years from now?

It has been an interesting thing for me in recent years to catalogue all of the references made by men of proven worth whenever they speak of men like Owen. Read Dabney, Thornwell, Alexander and other great preachers, and all of them again and again tip their hat to Owen, not as an erudite theologian, but as a man who conditioned their minds to be better preachers. Alexander says that his father's advice to him was "never go one day without reading at least five minutes in an author of the likes of Owen." It was his father's practice to read through volume 3 on the Holy Spirit at least once a year for the development and conditioning of a spiritually sensitive and pastorally oriented mind and spirit.

We want to learn how to be pleaders with the souls of men. I know the cavalier way in which some people dismiss Spurgeon's sermons: 'They are not exegetical, they are just topical.' Such people are common place little pip squeaks who couldn't preach their way out of a six by seven room made of balsa wood, in throwing out these little snide remarks at Spurgeon. Well, he may not be to us the best model of a Murray-like exegete. Let's take Professor Murray for our model of carefully reasoned exegesis. But if you've reached the place where you can't learn something about preaching from Spurgeon, and where your heart is not warmed by the pervasive Christological flavour that just oozes out of Spurgeon, something is wrong with you, friend! If you can't take Bunyan's Pilgrim's Progress and read through it with a view to learning what it is to preach and to go after the souls of men where they are, in all of their refuges of lies, then brethren you've gone too far! But I don't know of any theological seminaries that are making their students read Owen, Spurgeon or Bunyan with a view to learning from them. A student wouldn't appear respectable in the twentieth century if someone met him and asked: "Where do you go to college?" "Oh such and such." "Ah, what have been your reading assignments?" "Bunyan, Spurgeon, Owen, Thornwell."

If you want your soul to take fire, read Thornwell's

theological treatises. It is like being caught up into the third heaven; penetrating in insights, but warm. They exude the passion of the religious element. The same is true of Warfield, when he is not writing on some unusually technical theme. The religious element breathes through his writing, as it does in Calvin's Institutes.

Principle No. 5.

The authority and regulative influence of the church over the entire framework of specialised training ought never to be suspended or neutralised by any other structure. (The key text is 1 Timothy 3:15.) It is the church which is the pillar and the stay of the truth. Whatever ecclesiological view we hold; whether we think of the church in its broader sense in the Presbyterian concept, or in a more limited sense in the independent or Baptist concept, this much is true: the church is the pillar and stay of the truth. Therefore all students, all instructors, and the entire operation of the school, must be answerable to the God-ordained authority and influence of the church—and not just on paper.

If church history teaches us anything, it teaches us the judgment of God on the church when she has made her theological colleges a no-man's land of their own. The sluice-gates of the heresy which has inundated the churches were opened in the schools of theological training. And they were opened when the church effectively relinquished its control, other than on paper. The life, the doctrine, the conduct, the influence of every instructor ought to be as much under the scrutiny of the elders of the church as the lives of the students.

Well brethren, this latter topic could be opened up further, but those are my five theses, much short of Luther's ninety-five. I hope they will challenge you to think and to wrestle and, by the grace of God, may we yet see a new day dawn in the area of ministerial training by the Lord's help and power. Amen.

CHAPTER 3.

The Call and Commission
of the Preacher

In a very real sense, this theme is not a theme that is exclusively the concern of preachers. The church is to act biblically with respect to the call and commission of those on whom it will lay its hands for the work of the ministry. For those of you who are not preachers, and for those who have no aspirations to be preachers, this is not a matter of secondary concern. You are part of the church of Christ, and therefore must obey the Lord, who says that you and I are to pray the Lord of the harvest to send forth labourers into His harvest. You are indeed vitally concerned with the subject in hand; 'The Call and the Commission of the Preacher.'

Perpetuity of the Teaching Office
In order to set our meditation within a broad biblical framework, I wish briefly to comment upon several passages of the Word of God before opening

up the subject itself. The first one is 2 Timothy 2:2. Paul, writing to Timothy, and giving to him many duties with respect to the life and functioning of the churches, says: "the things which thou hast heard from me among many witnesses, the same commit thou to faithful men, who shall be able to teach others also." We may say in a very general sense that this text underscores the task of the church in the discovery and training of faithful men for the work of the ministry. Although it is Christ the Head of the church who gives pastors and teachers to the church, this text indicates that the church itself is responsible for the perpetuation of the teaching office. No matter how rich may be the teaching gifts deposited in our own individual assemblies, we must never be indifferent to this responsibility of the perpetuity of the teaching gift and of the teaching office.

Then in Romans 12, the apostle indicates that each of us has an individual responsibility with respect to discerning the nature of our own gifts. In this chapter in verse 3 the apostle, first of all warning against the sin of pride, that none is to think more highly of himself than he ought to think, then exhorts to a sober assessment with respect to our gifts. "For I say, through the grace that was given me, to every man that is among you, not to think of himself more highly than he ought to think; but so to think as to think soberly, according as God hath dealt to each man a measure of faith." Then, as he goes on to mention the unity of the body but diversity of gifts, he says in verse 6, "And having gifts differing according to the grace that was given unto us, whether prophecy, let us prophesy according to the proportion of our faith, or ministry, let us give ourselves to our ministry; or he that teacheth, to his teaching; or he that exhorteth to his exhorting." Not only does the church, according to 2 Timothy, have a responsibility for the perpetuity of the teaching office, but each of us has an individual responsibility to discern whether or not the Head of the church has endowed us with a gift that ought to be exercised for the work of the ministry.

In James 3:1 there is given a very sober warning to anyone who comes, at least tentatively, to the conclusion that he ought to fulfil the function of an official and public teacher in the church of Christ: "Be not many of you teachers, my brethren, knowing that we shall receive heavier judgment." For those who have some indication that the Lord may indeed be fashioning them into pastor-teachers and may be endowing them with the requisite gifts and graces for the work of the ministry, here is a word of sober caution: "be not many of you teachers, knowing that we shall receive heavier judgment."

Then in 1 Timothy 3:1, we have given to us both the encouragement and the standard for the work of the ministry: "Faithful is the saying", (and this is one of those five sayings that apparently had become, as it were, common sanctified clichés in the early church)—"Faithful is the saying, if any man seeketh

73

the office of a bishop" (an overseer, a pastor, a shepherd, an elder), "he desireth a good work. The bishop therefore must be . . ." Then there follows a description of balanced and practical godliness and also the requisite gifts for public ministry.

The Call and Commission

Now against this broad backdrop which, I trust, has convinced us that this subject is one of general concern to the people of God, we now want to come to grips with the vast and important issue of the Call and the Commission of the Preacher. As I address myself to this subject, I do so with great fear, because of two very real extremes into which men and women, fellows and girls have often fallen. There is first of all, the danger of going beyond the balanced teaching of Scripture, and thereby discouraging some men from pursuing the work of the ministry, who ought to pursue that work. We may set a standard that goes beyond Scripture and is so high that even good and gifted men feel that the standard is beyond them.

On the other hand, there is the very real danger of falling short of the balanced teaching of the Word of God, and thereby encouraging some to pursue and enter the work of the ministry whom the Lord has not equipped for this task. One of the most searching indictments in this realm is found in Ezekiel 13:22 where God speaks of the tragic effects of those who run without having been sent. Spurgeon was very conscious of this danger. When addressing himself to the whole subject of the call to the ministry, he said:

> "That is a weighty enquiry, and I desire to treat it most solemnly. O for divine guidance in so doing! That hundreds have missed their way, and stumbled against a pulpit is sorrowfully evident from the fruitless ministries and decaying churches which surround us. It is a fearful calamity to a man to miss his calling, and to the church upon whom he imposes himself, his mistake involves an affliction of the most grievous kind. It would be a curious and painful subject for reflection—the frequency with which men in the possession of reason mistake the end of their existence, and aim at objects which they were never intended to pursue."[1]

Spurgeon underscores the fact that it is no simple thing to come to a clearly settled conviction, based upon the Word of God, with respect to this great question: "Am I, or am I not, called to the work of the Christian ministry?"

In order to think our way through this subject, I propose first of all, to lay out three foundational principles which must be present to condition all of our thinking on this subject. It is an ignorant pew which produces a low standard of ministerial excellence. If those of you who sit in the pew begin to think biblically about what you will tolerate in the pulpit, maybe you will have something better in the pulpit as a result.

---

1. Spurgeon, C.H. "Lectures to My Students" Vol.1, Lect.ii.

Principle No. 1

There will be latitude and diversity in the application of the biblical principles involved in this matter of the call and commission of the preacher.

This subject falls into the realm of what we might call experimental or practical divinity or theology. Wherever the truth is brought to bear upon the experience of men and women, there you have experimental or practical divinity. The moment we enter the realm of experimental or practical divinity, we find that the ways of the Spirit of God are as they are in regeneration: the Lord Jesus said that the wind blows where it wills; you cannot tell where it comes from, or where it is going, but you hear the sound thereof.

When the Spirit of God is brooding over the heart and life of a man, forming him into an able minister of the new covenant, there is an element of inscrutability, an element of mystery, and an element of divine sovereignty in the pattern of the Holy Spirit's working. No two men are fashioned and called to the work of the ministry in precisely the same way. As I attempt to articulate the biblical principles I do not want anyone to assume that I am saying that those principles will always find a sameness in their application to each individual. There will be latitude and diversity in the application of the biblical principles relative to this matter of the call and commission of the preacher.

When I first began to study this subject in any

great depth, I tried to surround myself with the masters who wrote on the subject. It was interesting to me to see the tremendous spectrum of perspective on the subject. I would say that way over on the left hand is Spurgeon, with his poetic and mystical temperament. Spurgeon takes a position with regard to the call to the ministry that would exclude many of us from this call, and would exclude many who **ought** to be in the ministry. He wrote such statements as these: "If you can do anything else other than preach, then don't preach!" I do not think that there is any biblical support for such a statement. Spurgeon is very strong on the subjective element of a felt consciousness of the call of God—the 'divine seizure.'

On the other end of the spectrum which we might call the extreme right, is Dabney, who actually becomes sarcastic and lampoons this whole idea. He says "how is the young man to be struck with this arrow of the heavenly Cupid which will make him fall in love for a task which he has never experienced, and concerning which he is basically ignorant?" Dabney, without realising it, goes after Spurgeon and lays him in the dust. Between Spurgeon on the left and Dabney on the right, there is Thornwell, who is a few degrees toward the centre from Mr Spurgeon. Then there is John Newton, who is about dead centre. Finally, Edmund Clowney's excellent little book: "Called to the Ministry" has, I believe, struck even closer to the biblical view.

Why do I give you that information? Well, not to impress you that I have read a few books, but simply to underscore this very principle. Had these men been more careful to understand this principle, they would not have pontificated in the application of the general biblical principles. You and I must beware of any absolutising in the outworking of these principles.

Tradition

It is also obvious that most denominations develop a kind of orthodoxy with regard to what constitutes a call to the ministry. In some denominations, if you've not felt a flutter of the left ventricle at 3 o'clock in the morning, or if you've not heard the flutter of angels' wings at about 1.32 a.m., why, you're simply not called! In other circles, if you cannot demonstrate a very calm, rational and almost passionless conviction that has lead you to the idea that you ought to be a preacher, why, you are suspected of being a little bit too mystical and, perhaps, a little bit light between the ears! One encounters these different traditions within denominational circles. My plea therefore, is 'let us beware of absolutising the biblical principles in their outworking.'

Principle No. 2

We must approach this subject fully aware that we are considering the call and commission of a man to an ordinary office in the church, and not an extraordinary office.

What do I mean by the terms 'ordinary office' and 'extraordinary office'? Simply this. The offices of apostle, prophet and possibly, evangelist (that is a moot question), are extraordinary offices. There are no more prophets in the church today in the sense that Isaiah, Jeremiah and Ezekiel were prophets of the Old Testament, or John the Baptist and Agabus (the prophet who came down and predicted Paul's imprisonment and his trials at the hands of the Jews) were of the New Testament. That office is an extraordinary office.

Almost without exception, extraordinary offices were attended with extraordinary calls to the office. For example, consider Isaiah: "In the year that King Uzziah died I saw the Lord . . . I heard the voice of the Lord, saying, Whom shall I send, and who will go for us? Then said I, Here am I; send me" (Isa. 6:1, 8). Again, one day a man who is devoted to his parents and to his menial task of farming, is cutting a furrow in his quiet little village, when a strange man with a hairy mantle across his shoulders, stops by his plow and casts this mantle upon his shoulder. Then Elisha knows that he is called to the prophetic office. You see, the extraordinary office was almost invariably attended by an extraordinary call.

When we talk about the call and commission of the preacher, we are talking about an ordinary office in the church of Jesus Christ, and therefore we do not look for extraordinary means in the process of that call. Frankly, I am amazed at the de facto

79

pentecostalism that exists in the best of even Reformed circles. Let me illustrate. A young man comes with
a saintly look upon his face, an earnestness in his
voice, and says to his minister, "I believe the Lord is
calling me to the ministry." "Well, what makes you
think that?" "I've just had this sense in my spirit that
the Lord is calling me." Well, many people feel that
it is tantamount to blasphemy to ask the young man:
"Pray tell, whence this feeling? What is the basis of
this feeling? How do you know this feeling is the call
of God?" At least in our country, there are thousands
of young men in Bible schools and seminaries who
say, "God is calling me to the ministry", yet their
call consists in nothing more or less than this subjective itch somewhere in the psyche. And no one dares
question it! So it is nurtured by a pastor, then it is
nurtured by the instructors, and finally, the young
man graduates from Bible school or seminary. He
candidates (he 'preaches with a view', as our British
friends say, which means preaching with the possibility
of being called). Then the fruitless, barren, useless
ministry of years are mute testimony to the fact that
God never did call the man. God never laid his hand
upon him and endued him with the necessary gifts
and graces.

As we wrestle with this issue, let us do so with the
understanding that we are dealing with the call to an
ordinary office by ordinary means.

Principle No. 3

Thirdly, if we are to tread surely in this matter,

we must think of the call of the ministry primarily in terms of the call to the office of an elder. Until we begin to think in such a way as to have our thinking dominated by 1 Timothy chapter 3 and Titus chapter 1, we will not think biblically concerning the call and commission of a man to the work of the ministry.

This may sound unbelievable to some of you, I hope not; but I have actually sat on ordination councils which examined men with respect to their call to the ministry where 1 Timothy 3 and Titus 1 were not so much as even opened and read in the entire process, let alone made the framework of examination. One minister was assigned to examine the candidate in his doctrine of God, someone else examined him in his ecclesiology, and another in his soteriology and his eschatology. He was examined on this, that and the other, but never once was 1 Timothy 3 or Titus 1 opened, and the following questions asked: "Young man, do you aspire to the office of an elder?" "Yes esteemed brethren, I do." "Are you prepared to submit yourself to the scrutiny of the divine standard?"

Many a pulpit committee meets and draws up its list of what it is looking for in a new pastor, and this passage is never even opened. It is not even consulted! Various candidates meet with these pulpit committees, and everything under the sun is discussed except the word of King Jesus with respect to His standards! The call and commission of the preacher is not even considered. Brothers and sisters, this ought not so to be!

There needs to be in all our hearts a renewed determination that to us the Kingship of Christ will be more than an abstraction and that His throne rights in this subject will be duly recognised by thinking scripturally. The call and commission of the preacher is essentially the recognition of the activity of Jesus Christ, the head of the church, in equipping a man with the gifts and graces outlined in 1 Timothy 3 and in Titus chapter 1.

Indispensable Elements

There are three indispensable, irreducable elements of a biblical call to the pastoral office.

1. The first is obvious from 1 Timothy 3:1. It is the presence of **desire born of right motives**. "Faithful is the saying, if a man seeketh the office of a bishop he desireth a good work." Tying this in with Peter's words, "Exercising the oversight thereof, not of constraint, but willingly" (1 Peter 5:2), none should ever be set apart for the work of the ministry who is not conscious of a desire for the work.

Notice the language: "If any man desireth" (or seeketh) "the office of a bishop, he desireth a good work." It is not a matter of someone having a romantic notion of some apparent place of position and influence and attention and public attraction. No! There is to be a desire for the work, for the labour of the ministry, and that desire must have become, to some degree, an element of spiritual obsession. The language in this text is strong: "If any man seeketh (if any man stretches out after) the office of a bishop, he desires (he lusts after) a good work." By the use of these two words the apostle focuses on this indispensable element of a biblical call.

Thornwell has some very perceptive things to say with respect to this element. It is indicative of the work of the Head of the church who is Himself implanting this yearning, this desire, this longing, for the work to which He Himself is calling him. But it must be emphasised that these desires are to be born of right motives, motives that are biblically realistic, motives that are spiritual in nature, motives framed by truth and produced by the Holy Spirit.

What are some of the motives?

The first would be a burning desire to serve the people of God unto their edification. 1 Corinthians 14 makes it very evident that the end for which all gifts of public ministry are given is the edification of the body of Christ. In a real sense, the ministry is a perpetual diaconal service. Jesus said, "I am among you as he that serveth." Those with even a cursory acquaintance with the language of the New Testament, know that the verb "to serve" is the word from which we get our word deacon. Jesus was saying: 'I am among you as he that serveth. He that would be great among you, let him become servant of all.'

Though Scripture makes it abundantly clear that there is a functional difference between the elder (presbyter), the bishop (episcopos) and the deacon, that difference is in the capacity of their office. In terms of spirit and attitude, there is no difference. The work of an elder is a constant work of diaconal service. We are to reflect the spirit of our Master who said, "I came not to be ministered unto, but to minister" (that is, to deacon, to serve) "and to give my life a ransom for many." When a man begins to aspire to the office of the ministry with a motive to serve the people of God unto their edification, then there is some indication that indeed the Head of the church is fashioning him into an able minister of the New Covenant.

A second element of proper motives would be that of burning desire to be used of God in that primary means ordained of God to call out His elect—the foolishness of "preaching". That word not only points in the direction of content, but in the direction of method. God has ordained that men will be saved by the foolishness of the thing preached. We have the classic passages in Romans 10, "Faith cometh by hearing, and hearing by the Word of God" (KJV), and "How shall they hear without a preacher?" Then there is that wonderful statement, "How beautiful are the feet of them that bring glad tidings of good things!"

When a man begins to feel, borne within his own heart, a longing to be used of God as that primary means of calling out his sheep, then indeed there is some indication that the Lord is calling him to this work.

Another element of a proper motive is that burning desire to discharge one's stewardship. Paul could say in 1 Corinthians 9:16, 17 (and I paraphrase here), 'a stewardship is laid upon me. It's no big deal if I preach! Necessity is laid upon me; woe is me if I preach not.'

Some of these elements of motive will be stronger in some men than others. Some will seem to develop at an earlier stage. Again I would try to make plain that I am not absolutising about the order of these things or the intensity of them. Again I would underscore, in the light of 1 Timothy 3, that if anyone is being formed of Christ into an able minister of the New Covenant, one of the first indications will be found here. There will be desire born of proper motives.

2. **Mature Christian Experience.** Added to the presence of desire born of right motives, the second category which indicates the Lord's working in preparing a man and fashioning him for the ministry, is the presence of those graces of character, indicative of genuine, balanced, and matured Christian experience. Continuing in 1 Tim. 3:2 do we read: 'A bishop therefore must be a man with an IQ of 150?' Or perhaps 'The bishop therefore must be a man with a massive library; one who can engage in lengthy theological disputes?' No, No! Having dealt with the presence of proper motive and desire, the Apostle then zeroes in on this whole subject of

genuine, balanced and matured Christian experience. "The bishop therefore must be without reproach . . .", that is, there must be no just cause to censure his life.

What does it mean to be without reproach? I say to you preachers, here is one of the great justifications or mandates for specific applicatory preaching. Some claim: "well, I state the truth in general and I allow the Holy Ghost to apply it." That is nonsense! You have to throw out half your Bible if you claim this. Paul doesn't say 'the works of the flesh are manifest and you know what they are; now let's get onto other business.' He says, "the works of the flesh are manifest, which are these . . ." Then he lists a whole bunch and says in effect, 'and that's not the end of the list' when he adds "and such like". So he doesn't say that the bishop therefore must be blameless, and then lets it go at that. He then exegetes what it means to be blameless. The bishop must be without reproach.

Paul starts first of all with the domestic: "The husband of one wife, temperate, soberminded, orderly, given to hospitality." Next, he mentions the one that deals with gifts, "an apt teacher." Then he goes back to character, "no brawler, no striker but gentle, not contentious, no lover of money, one that ruleth well his own house, having his children in subjection with all gravity." This latter characteristic Paul amplifies in a parenthetical question: "For if a man know not how to rule his own house, how shall he take care of the church of God?" Returning

86

to the list he stipulates "not a novice", that is a recent convert, lest being lifted up with pride, "he fall into the condemnation of the devil. Moreover he must have good testimony from them that are without; lest he fall into reproach and the snare of the devil." Now when you bring together everything that is said in this list of practical evidences of godliness, what do you have? Simply a picture of genuine, balanced, matured Christian experience, which the apostle says must, of necessity, be present before a man is ever called and set apart for the work of the ministry.

"The bishop therefore must be . . .", says Paul. He is very careful to give us specimens of godliness in various dimensions of human relationships. There are some men who are quite self controlled when it comes to their physical appetites for food, sex, and so on. They may be relatively sober minded, but they are not orderly. They are scatterbrains. They have no sense of organisation. They waste hours because they are not orderly men. The apostle says such a one is not qualified for this office as long as that deficiency is not rectified.

Furthermore, 1 Tim. 3:4 assumes that a bishop will be a married man with children, though not necessarily so. What is emphasised is that if he is a married man, he must rule well his own house. That is, he must know that fusion of authority graced with gentleness. He must know how to give authoritative directions without being a tyrant. He must know how to be gentle without being un-principled, lest his household be ungoverned. Why? Because in a sense the church is nothing but a large household, with little babies that cry for their bottles and teenagers that are out to run the show, and buck against everything under the sun. (I'm not talking about chronological categories, I'm talking about spiritual categories). There are old people with arthritis not only in their physical joints, but in their mental and spiritual joints. Every time you try to take them one foot further than they've gone before in their understanding, they cry "Oh my arthritis! Oh my arthritis!"

An elder's testimony must be good without, in the place where he works, in the way he drives his car, and in the way he pays his bills. Isn't it tragic that preachers are notorious for two things: having houses full of brats, and being utterly indifferent to speed limits. Brethren, we laugh, but isn't that tragic in the light of this passage? A good testimony from those that are without is essential. How can we call men to obey the law of God when we stand to preach in the house of God, when we disobey that law when we get out into our cars. 'Obey every ordinance of man for the Lord's sake' is the biblical principle, and that speed limit is an ordinance of man! Why are preacher's children notorious for their bratishness, when God says that if a man does not rule well his own house he has no business ruling the house of God?

3. Gifts for Edification. In this whole matter of the call and commission of the preacher, it is essential that we understand that if we are to act biblically, we must act first of all with these convictions, that we need to see men in whom there is desire born of right motives, secondly, the presence of graces of character indicative of balanced, matured Christian experience, and thirdly, there must be the evidence of gifts necessary for the edification of the people of God. This third point we shall now consider.

The language of 1 Timothy 3 is clear. The elder must be an apt teacher; or in the language of the parallel passage in Titus 1, he must be one who holds "to the faithful word which is according to the teaching, that he may be able both to exhort in the sound doctrine and to convict the gainsayers." You see, he must not only have a grasp upon the truth, but the ability to convey the truth, with conviction and with convincing authority.

The assumption so often held in our day, is this: if a man's mind has the ability to absorb and retain truth, he then must automatically have some commensurate ability to convey that truth to the minds of others. But the two do not necessarily meet in every man. I think of the incident recorded in James Stewart's excellent little book on preaching. (By recommending that little book, I'm not recommending him as a theologian or recommending him in other areas, but his little book on preaching has some excellent material). A young man came to him one day and said, "Dr Stewart, I'm wondering if you can help me." He said, "well son if I can I'd be glad to." "I just don't know what's wrong with my preaching. It just doesn't seem to be coming through to my people. Can you help me?" "Well, I'll tell you what I want you to do," Dr Stewart said. "Now I'm going to sit here as though I were a member of your congregation, and for the next twenty minutes I want you to preach to me the sermon you preached to them yesterday." So with some degree of reserve and fearfulness, understandably so, the young man attempted to preach his sermon to Dr Stewart. When he was through, he said, "Well what are your thoughts, sir?" "Precisely this", replied Dr Stewart. "Young man, for twenty minutes you have been desperately trying to get something out of your head, instead of spending twenty minutes putting something into mine."

Do you see what his problem was? He was not an apt teacher. He could not take the body of knowledge that he had learned, and by the skilful use of all the tools of communication, get it into the head of his hearer. If that ability is not there or cannot be cultivated by prayer and pains, no amount of knowledge or piety will make up for its deficiency. A man must be an apt teacher. He must not only hold to the faithful word, but he must be able with that faithful word, to exhort and to convict. He must be able so to speak, as to build up the saint and to explode the fallacy of the one who holds error.

We read in Ephesians chapter 4 that the great Head of the church gives gifts to his church, among them pastors and teachers. The activity of Christ in giving such gifts is seen in the presence of the gifts. John Owen has one of the most penetrating and perceptive comments on this that I found anywhere in any uninspired literature. He asks, "how can we know if a man is a gift of Christ to the church?" He answers, "Well, by this simple rule of thumb. If those gifts are given for the edification of the saints or perfecting of the saints unto the work of the ministry, then wherever such gifts as will build up the church are present, Christ has given a gift to his church. Where the gift is absent in terms of its ability to edify, Christ has not given a gift to the church."

That sounds so simple, yet it is profound in its implications. Milton's words have not lost their force in our own generation: "Hungry sheep look up and are not fed." I am not speaking of congregations that become overly fastidious, and want the truth of God served up in excellence. They want in their Pastor all the fire and passion of a Whitefield, all the exegetical skills of a Professor Murray, all of the commanding presence and voice of a Dr Martyn Lloyd-Jones, and all of the everything of everyone else who has been a preacher of any worth! There are people like that, but I am not talking of those people. I am talking about dear saints who come prayerfully to the house of God; who come prepared to think, and to give themselves to the ministry of

91

the Word. But it would take a gift that I don't even know is described in the Bible for them to be able to sort out the head and the tail of Dr Stewart's poor man's sermon, to find out where he was and where he is going and where he intended to be when he got there. This goes on week after week after week!

There is a biblical call to the ministry where there is the evidence that God has given the necessary gifts to edify the people of God. This is why a proven ability to teach and to preach sound doctrine, and a proven ability to rule and govern, are absolutely essential if a man is to know that he is truly called of the living God to the work of the ministry.

Who Decides?

In conclusion, let me address myself to this very vital question: By whom are these things to be discovered? Who is to determine whether or not are present the desires born of right motives, the balanced proven godliness of character and the gifts necessary unto edification? By whom are these graces and gifts to be discerned? Well, obviously to some degree, by the one who aspires to the work of the ministry. Who knoweth the things of a man save the spirit of a man which is in him? Who can tell if those desires to be used of God as an instrument of edification become a burning conviction, but the man in whom they are becoming a burning conviction? So these gifts and graces and desires must to some degree be discerned by the one who aspires to the office. Consider Romans 12:2 again. Every one of you, Paul says, is to judge soberly. I have an obligation, you have an obligation, to enter into a period of serious self-examination in the presence of God with respect to potential gifts and ability for the work of the ministry.

In great measure these things are to be discerned by the people of God, walking under the discipline and rule of the Word of God, not under the discipline and pressure of sentimental notions.

Unbiblical Approaches

There's that dear soul who, before her child was ever born, prayed that she would bring a preacher into the world. From the time she dandled her lovely little boy upon her knee, she always viewed him as her preacher. She let him know that, and she has conditioned his conscience and his whole psychological makeup to believe that if he doesn't go into the ministry, he'll break his mother's heart and frustrate the end for which he was conceived and brought into the world—and many other ills. I have met such men; twisted, warped, useless men.

This matter of the church discerning whether or not God's hand is on a man, is to be a discerning that is born, not of sentiment or of personal desire, but of a careful adherence to the clear teaching of the Word of God. It is not to grow out of what I call the 'ministerial status symbol'. With some preachers, every time a young man says he feels called to the ministry, it is like putting a notch in their rifle. I have been in the presence of men who say with a very forced look of humility, "well you know God has really blessed in recent days, we have six men preparing for the ministry." Outwardly they say this, but inwardly they notch up another catch. This is an easy thing to do, my brethren. When you have been used of God to influence a young man for the kingdom of God, you have a powerful influence upon that man. I am not saying that you do not have an obligation to challenge him with respect to the work of the ministry; to press upon him the sober responsibility and to plead with God as to whether or not God would furnish him with the gifts and graces to be used in the work of the ministry. I do not believe we are to be totally passive in this matter, but neither are we to pressure people in such a way as to promote our own pride. These gifts and graces are to be discovered by the individual, and by the church with its God-ordained leadership, thinking and acting by the rule of the Word of the living God.

Blessings

What a wonderful thing it is to have men commended to us whose home churches have seen them, over past years, develop in grace and in gift until the church, walking by the rule of Scripture, has come to the conviction that the Head of the church has His hand upon this man. Then they write and say, "will you please take them for a time, give them some of the tools that we're not equipped to give them, and watch over their souls for a period of time." These young men then come (and some are not so young—we must get away from this notion that it is only young men). Most of the men have already made it in business. They have nothing to prove. They were competent men, diligent with their hands to the plow of their secular employment. It became more and more evident as they served God's people that God's people saw in them gifts and graces and began to encourage them. Their elders encouraged them, so that they now have set their faces to the work of the ministry, with the conviction that this is not some nebulous notion spun out of the stuff of their own ideas. It is the conviction that the Head of the church is making his will known not only to the individual man, but to the whole church. Therefore they enter this solemn task in the confidence that they are truly called of God, and the day will come when that call will come to its wonderful expression, when the hands of the office bearers of a given church will be laid upon them, and they will solemnly declare that the Head of the church has furnished them with the gifts and graces requisite to the edification of the people of God.

A Final Plea

I plead with you who form the rank and file of God's people; who form the backbone of churches represented. Plead with God that you will think scripturally concerning this subject of the call and commission of the preacher. For you men who are elders, whether you perform in that office as teachers, or whether your primary task is that of ruling, may

God grant that together we will think scripturally and dare to begin some radical scriptural pursuit of these principles.

Somebody has got to be willing somewhere, at sometime, to cut through the rubbish of tradition and dare to be biblical. I trust such a group of men will hear this plea. If you want a good little bibliography that will help sharpen your thinking on some of these things, I will close this lecture with these suggestions: In Charles Bridges' *The Christian Ministry,* two excellent sections may be found in pages 24-31 and 90-102. In Robert Lewis Dabney's *Discussions Evangelical and Theological* Vol.2, there is an essay entitled 'A Call to the Ministry'.

Charles Spurgeon's *Lectures to My Students* also includes a chapter entitled 'The Call to the Ministry'. Dr Edmund P. Clowney has written an excellent book *Called to the Ministry* (IVP). Other helpful material may be found in John Owen's Works, Vol.9, page 452f and Vol.16 pages 74-90. Finally, James Henley Thornwell's Works Vol.4 pages 15-42 contain excellent material. These have been a great help in sharpening my own thinking on this matter.

Some of you may be thinking, "well, if we implement standards like this, we'll clear half the existing ministers, empty out three-quarters of our theological colleges, and what will happen?" I will close with a quote from my good companion Gardner Spring, who answered a question similar to this:

"I answer, in the first place, it must be by a watchful

eye over the young men who are pursuing their theological education. The rivalship of numbers is unworthy of these seats of sacred science."

What he was saying is that when theological colleges are pushing for enrolment it is a shame.

"Numbers may ruin us. It is impossible that a very large number of students should enjoy that pastoral supervision which they need. Many a young man has finished his course in our theological seminaries, who never ought to have thought of the ministry, and whom a faithful pastoral supervision would have so instructed; while more have suffered in their usefulness as ministers for the want of that personal inspection which, from the multitude of students, it has been impossible to exercise."

Now hear his classic statement:

"Give us abler, better and more spiritual preachers, even if they be fewer. The three hundred that lapped under Gideon were more potent than the mighty host of Midian. May God grant us a Gideon's band of men truly called and equipped of the Head of the church, to do this awesome task of the work of the ministry."

Amen.

CHAPTER 4.

The Devotional Life
of the Preacher

The apostle Paul, speaking to Timothy himself as a man and as a minister, charges him with these words: "Let no man despise thy youth; but be thou an example to them that believe, in word, in manner of life, in love, in faith, in purity. Till I come give heed to reading, to exhortation, to teaching. Neglect not the gift that is in thee, which was given thee by prophecy, with the laying on of the hands of the presbytery. Be diligent in these things; give thyself wholly to them; that thy progress may be manifest unto all. Take heed [or pay close and constant attention] to thyself and to thy teaching. Continue in these things; for in doing this thou shalt save both thyself and them that hear thee" (1 Tim. 4:12-16).

In order that there be no misunderstanding on this subject, let me first of all define what I mean throughout the entire study, when I use the term, "the devotional life" of the preacher. From a negative standpoint I am not assuming or inferring that a man's life is divided into the secular and the sacred, as though he is more holy or pleasing to God when he is in prayer than when he is out playing cricket or soccer with his son, or shining the shoes of his children on a Saturday night prior to the Lord's Day.

When we speak of the devotional life of the preacher, we are speaking of a specific kind of activity. I do not speak of that activity out of a context which places a dichotomy between the secular and the sacred. Rather, in using the expression "the devotional life of the preacher," I am referring specifically to the minister's acts and habits of secret prayer and private meditative reading of the Scriptures and related literature, for the express purpose of the development of his own spiritual life with no conscious reference to his particular public ministerial duties.

Spiritual Sustenance

In other words, in contemplating the pastor's devotional life, we are considering the preacher at prayer; not primarily because he is a preacher, but because he is a Christian who must pray, in order to sustain his own spiritual life. We are contemplating him pouring over the Scriptures, not because he must analyse and proclaim these Scriptures to others as food for their souls, but because as a Christian man, he desires to feed his own soul upon the Bread of Life.

Typically, we might find him reading some of the

more devotional authors or portions of the literature of men who are known for more than just their devotional import. For example, he may be reading Flavel on *Keeping the Heart,* not to construct sermons for his people, but in order to keep his own heart. In order to make progress in his own mortification of sin, he may be reading volume six of the Works of John Owen. In order to be a more spiritually minded man, he may be reading Owen, volume seven. I hope that this has made it sufficiently clear as to what we are dealing with in considering the pastor's devotional life.

As we think our way through this unspeakably important subject I want to follow several lines of thought. First of all, I want to address myself to the importance of the pastor's devotional life. Then secondly I want to consider some hindrances to the pastor's devotional life, and point out the pathway to a fruitful pastoral devotional life.

1. The Importance of the Pastor's Devotional Life.

First of all, I would like to consider the general principle. In 1 Tim. 4:16, the apostle Paul says to Timothy in a present imperative: 'Be continually paying close attention to **yourself.**' Then, after this, he adds 'to your teaching'. In other words, amidst all of the duties which Paul had laid upon him (and there were many arduous and time-consuming responsibilities), Timothy must pay constant, careful attention to himself.

Paul is not content to give a charge in the present

imperative. He then, as it were, buttresses that charge with the further exhortation, 'continue in these things.' Timothy's life was not to be a matter of fits and starts. Paul is not speaking of coming to a conference and having your conscience plowed up, concerning prayerlessness; or of having your spirit disturbed concerning the absence of the devotional assimilation of Scripture; and then for a few weeks or days, giving yourself with some degree of enthusiasm to this task. No, no! Paul commands Timothy to continue in these things. This is precisely the order that the apostle gives to the Ephesian elders. In Acts 20:28, as he addresses these elders of the church with respect to their God-given duties, he says: "Take heed unto yourselves, and to all the flock, in which the Holy Spirit hath made you bishops, to feed the church of God which he purchased with his own blood."

What is the first and primary duty of these Ephesian elders? To take heed unto themselves. This exhortation occurs in the midst of the announced reality of the presence of heresy and error from without and within, amidst all the other tasks involved in shepherding the flock of God. These elders were to view this task as one which had as its primary focal point, the nurture and cultivation of their own walk with the living God.

The Commandments

We may also relate it to the structure of the commandments when our Lord was asked, "which is the first and great commandment?" He answered, "the first and greatest commandment is, thou shalt love the Lord thy God with all thy heart, mind, soul and strength, and the second is like unto it, thou shalt love thy neighbour as thyself." In the work of the ministry we are performing the duties of the second table of the law. We are ministering to our fellow men. But the first commandment is the first in importance.

We must never so serve our neighbours as to undercut those disciplines essential to the nurturing of our own love to the living God. As one has said, "the life of a man's ministry is the life of the minister." If the life of a minister is the life of his ministry, then the very soul of his life is his own devotional exercises. If it is true that out of the abundance of the heart the mouth speaketh, then the most necessary preparation for the formal disciplines of oral ministry is the nurture of the heart. "Guard thy heart above all that thou guardest, for out of it are the issues of life." So the importance of a pastor's devotional life can be seen first of all, in the light of this general principle which I have articulated from these texts.

Confirming Spiritual Experience

Now let me suggest four specific aspects of the importance of maintaining a fruitful devotional life, as a pastor. It is important, first of all, in confirming the reality of our professed spiritual experience. Notice that I said 'confirming', not 'imparting'.

Brethren, as long as Matthew 7:21-23 exists in Scripture, we must always remember that there is a frightening possibility that a man may have great ministerial gifts and abounding ministerial success, but be utterly devoid of saving and sanctifying grace! Our Lord said in that sobering passage, "Many will say unto me in that day, Lord, Lord, have we not prophesied in thy name, and in thy name cast out demons, and in thy name done many mighty works?" Our Lord does not debate their claims. He responds by saying, "Depart from me, I never knew you, you workers of iniquity." In other words, they had ministerial gifts and manifest success, but they were devoid of saving grace.

Few things are a more accurate index of the absence of saving grace than the absence of those spiritual disciplines in which the soul has direct engagement with God. One of the things which troubles me with that text is that it is in the same section in which Jesus, speaking of the broad road which leads to destruction, says, "many are they which enter in thereat." In the same context he says, "Many will say in that day" (and that does not refer to liberals), "we have preached in thy name." That is their claim. They recognised in Jesus of Nazareth the revelation of Jehovah, that God's name was in Him. Furthermore, He was not speaking to liberals, because liberals don't believe in the demonic. They explain everything in terms of psychology. They do not believe in the supernatural agency of the

Holy Spirit impinging directly upon the human personality and ridding that personality of a false spirit of hell called a demon. No liberal will therefore make that claim in the last day!

This is orthodox terminology: ". . . preached in thy name, in thy name cast out demons, and in thy name done many mighty works of powers" (the standard word for the miraculous). Liberals don't believe in the miraculous. My brethren, only orthodox preachers will make that claim, and Jesus said that there will be a host of them: **"Many** will say to me in that day . . ."

Few things are more telling in confirming the reality of vital spiritual life (or in exposing its absence!) than those disciplines connected with the pastor's devotional life.

True Sonship

What is it that characterises the child of God above all else? What is it that marks him out as totally unique? Is it not such qualities as those described in texts such as Phil. 3:3–"We are the true circumcision who worship by the Spirit of God, who glory in Christ Jesus and who put no confidence in the flesh"? Any man who is of the true circumcision, whose heart has been circumcised by the Holy Ghost, worships in the Spirit. In other words he has tasted the reality of felt communion with the living God. Having tasted that reality, his worship is something more than a reading of the rubric of the Prayer Book, or a mere mouthing of the phrases that he has absorbed in his evangelical tradition. We are the circumcision who worship God in the Spirit. In other words, our worship is spiritual in character. It has dimensions of vitality and perspective which only God the Holy Ghost can give.

Then there is the consequence of glorying in Christ Jesus. The spirit of prophecy is the spirit or the testimony of Jesus. Where there is worship in the Spirit there will be this preoccupation, this fixation, with Christ Jesus, a fixation that cannot be in any way satisfied by simply naming his name in public, by bringing his name in as an appendage to a prayer in the public disciplines of the ministry. There must be something of that inward longing for the fragrance of His presence which distils upon the heart in the secret place. Those who glory in Christ Jesus find a light in all that He is in the uniqueness of His Person, and in the perfection of His work, and therefore put no confidence in the flesh. In the context, it means no confidence in the flesh for acceptance before God in the matter of justification, but surely it is not limited to that. It is conditioned by it, but not limited by it. When I have been stripped of every last refuge as far as the ground of my acceptance before God, if I have seen that I am nothing, can do nothing but sin, and have nothing to commend myself to God, that disposition carries over into my total perspective of life.

I know that I carry within me the remains of corruption, a veritable tinderbox ready to break out

105

into a conflagration of the foulest sins imaginable. Therefore, having no confidence in the flesh, I will be often at the throne of grace praying, "O my Father, lead me not into temptations, subdue my passions, discipline my pride, harness my impetuosity!" At the throne of grace, I will have much business that has nothing to do with the church bell at eleven o'clock on Sunday morning.

The Hypocrite

Hear Jonathan Edwards, in his searching sermon on hypocrites deficient in the duties of secret prayer:

> "When a hypocrite hath had his false conversion, his wants are in his sense of things already supplied, his desires are already answered; and so he finds no further business at the throne of grace. He never was sensible that he had any other needs, but a need of being safe from hell. And now that he is converted, as he thinks, that need is supplied. Why then should he still go on to resort to the throne of grace with earnest requests? He is out of danger; all that he was afraid of is removed: he hath got enough to carry him to heaven, and what more should he desire?–While under awakenings, he had this to stir him up to go to God in prayer, that he was in continual fear of hell. But since in his own opinion he is converted, he hath no further business about which to go to God. And although he may keep up the duty of prayer in the outward form a little while, for fear of spoiling his hope, yet he will find it a dull business to continue it without necessity, and so by degrees he will let drop the practice. The work of the hypocrite is done when he is converted, and therefore he standeth in no

further need of help."[1]

Searching words are they not, my brother? Whereas the hypocrite may pray only so much as is necessary to pacify his conscience that he is converted, the unconverted minister may pray only so much as is necessary as to salve his conscience that he is an evangelical minister. But of that prayer that is born of the pressure of unfulfilled longing to commune with God, he knows nothing. Of that prayer which is born of the pressure for felt communion with Christ he knows nothing. Of that prayer that is wrung from a heart conscious of the terrible fomenting of the pressure of indwelling sin, he knows nothing.

My preacher friend, if you know nothing of devotional exercises, that is, secret prayer and meditative reflective reading of the Word of God with no conscious reference to official public ministerial duties, this could well be the index of your true spiritual state. I would be a fool to assume that every man at this Conference (or every reader—ed.) is truly in Christ. When I stand before God I want my hands to be clean of your blood, and I would sound this note with all earnestness, my friend. Is this perhaps the key to your chronic prayerlessness, that you have never tasted and felt the reality of true union with Jesus Christ?

Again and again, Whitefield speaks in his journals of ministers whom he was convinced were preaching

---

1. Edwards, Jonathon. Works, Vol.2, p.73 (B. of T. 1974)

an unfelt Christ. What was he talking about? This very thing. For it is by the Word of God that we see the face of our Saviour: ". . . we all, with unveiled face beholding as in a mirror the glory of the Lord" (2 Cor. 3:18). Our Lord is mirrored in the Scriptures, and therefore we turn to them as naturally as I turn morning and night to the pictures that are on my little desk in my room. Wherever I go, the first thing that comes out of my satchel is that envelope with the pictures of my wife and my children. Something of what they are and what they mean to me is reflected on that little piece of photographic paper. I don't need some one to knock on my door twice a day and say, "have you had your picture time?" The whole idea is ridiculous that people must be pressured with "Have you had your Quiet Time?"

Where the soul is taken up with the glory of Christ, there is that instinctive longing to behold His face. So then, the importance of the pastor's devotional life is seen, not only in the light of the general principle, but in the light of this first specific thing. It confirms the reality of the professed spiritual experience.

Maintaining Spiritual Life

Secondly, the pastor's devotional life is important in maintaining the vitality of his spiritual life, not only in confirming the reality of the professed life, but in maintaining the vitality of that life. Psalm 1 beautifully describes the man in Christ. Ultimately, it is a picture of the Lord Jesus Himself, the only one who perfectly eschewed the counsel of the ungodly; who never in heart or in affection found himself sitting in the way of the scoffers, and whose delight is in the law of the Lord, and on His law does he meditate day and night. In other words, his dealings with the Scriptures are not professional or intermittent. The Word of God has become to him what the water is to the roots of a tree planted by the riverside; the constant source of his nourishment and of his life. Jeremiah expressed this so beautifully when he said, "Thy words were found, and I did eat them; and thy Word was unto me the joy and rejoicing of my heart . . ." (Jer. 15:16).

You see, it is in the maintenance of this devotional assimilation of the Word of God that the vitality and the virility of spiritual life is sustained. It is here that the promises glow with a heavenly light that sweetens the spirit. It is here that the warnings thunder into our own spirit: "Moreover by them", David says, "is thy servant warned." Here the comforts distil like dew upon our parched hearts. Sin is revealed in the light of God's countenance. Heaven and eternity are brought near. Perspective is sharpened. The psalmist in Psalm 73 said that everything was confused. Nothing made sense until he went into the sanctuary of God. So if our spiritual lives are to be maintained with vitality, they must be maintained in these devotional exercises. Hear Bridges at this point:

> "But time must be found for the spiritual feeding upon Scriptural truths, as well as for a critical investigation of their meaning, or for a Ministerial

application of their message."

Notice the categories: Critical investigation of their meaning, ministerial application of their message and another dimension—spiritual feeding upon Scriptural truths.

> "For if we should study the Bible more as Ministers than as Christians—more to find matter for the instruction of our people, than food for the nourishment of our own souls; we neglect to place ourselves at the feet of our Divine Teacher; our communion with Him is cut off; and we become mere formalists in sacred profession . . . We cannot live by feeding others; or heal ourselves by the mere employment of healing our people."

Isn't that a profound statement? 'We cannot feed ourselves by feeding others, or heal ourselves by the mere employment of healing our people.' Bridges continues:

> " . . . and therefore by this course of official service our familiarity with the awful realities of death and eternity may be rather like that of the grave digger, the physician, and the soldier, than of the man of God, viewing eternity with deep seriousness and concern, and bringing to his people the profitable fruit of his contemplations. It has well been remarked—that 'when once a man begins to view religion not as of personal, but merely of professional importance, he has an obstacle in his course, with which a private Christian is unacquainted.' It is indeed difficult to determine, whether our familiar intercourse with the things of God is more our temptation or our advantage."[2]

---

2. Bridges, Charles. "The Christian Ministry" pp.162-163 (Banner of Truth, 1967)

Brethren, the men who begin well in the flush of their new found faith, in the vigour and the virility of conscious, vibrant communion with Christ, and who carry that through with an ever deepening, widening channel of spiritual vigour to the end of their days, are few and far between. Horatius Bonar remarks that there are few who maintain their vigour to the end. Brethren, this frightens me. As I have entered my middle years it has caused me much searching of heart and much earnest prayer. My prayer has been again and again, "Lord don't let me peter out. Take me now while there is still some freshness and vigour. Don't let me coast on the impetuousness of past days, and lose the reality and vitality of communion with Yourself, and the felt awareness of the world of spiritual reality."

Brethren, this danger is very real—particularly when we are committed to lengthy pastorates. When we see the same faces week by week, we can go through the same round of duties on mere conditioned reflex, like one of Pavlov's dogs. I plead with you, as I plead with my own heart, to maintain the disciplines of the devotional life at any cost; not only for the constant confirmation of the reality of our religion, but for the constant maintenance of the vitality of our spiritual lives.

Anointed Ministry

A healthy devotional life is important thirdly, because it provides the soil of an anointed ministry. Consistency in devotional disciplines alone provides the soil of an anointed ministry. If you want an interesting discussion the next time you get together with a group of preachers, introduce this question: "What is unction in preaching?" The closest I ever came to hearing a good answer was when that question was asked in a group of rural Southern black preachers. After much discussion, finally one of of them said, "Well brethren, I don't knows what unction is, but I knows what it aint!" I don't know if we can go much further than that!

Unction is that peculiar element of Divine energy that rests upon a man and upon his utterances, so that when he speaks you know that you are having dealings, not with another mere mortal, but you are having dealings with his God. The manner of his speaking may be very unanimated or it may contain the most intense forms of animated speech. He may be quiet or he may bellow. Unction has nothing to do with the externals and the incidentals of the manner of delivery. Unction is that peculiar something, in which God sits on a man's words when they leave his mouth, and when they strike our ears and hearts, we know that we are having dealings with the Almighty. That is unction, the soil of an anointed ministry. A ministry that has that unction is a ministry that is characterised by the language of the the apostle: "my speech and preaching was not with enticing words of men's wisdom, but in demonstration of the Spirit and of power" (1 Cor. 2:4). What elements of Divine sovereignty, and the inscrutability

112

of God's own will, enter (and they certainly do enter) our hearts!

By and large, the men who have known unction as the pattern of their ministries through the years, are men who knew the discipline of consistent devotional exercises. This is not capricious or arbitrary, though God is absolutely sovereign. It is because of this delicate relationship between secret meditative reading of the Word and the work of the Spirit, that unction is tied in with the devotional exercises of the preacher. We have read Luke 11 in our early morning prayer meeting today. It contains that wonderful passage in which our Lord says, "If ye then, being evil, know how to give good gifts unto your children; how much more shall your heavenly Father give the Holy Spirit to them that ask Him?" There is the relationship between our asking and His giving. Paul states in a striking manner in Phil. 1:19— "I know that this shall turn to my salvation through your prayer and the supply of the Spirit of Jesus Christ." Paul linked the prayer of the Philippians with the supply of the Spirit of Jesus Christ; while he himself was there in a Roman jail! Here is that deep and intimate relationship between prayer and the supply of the Spirit.

Seeking Unction

It is granted that we turn away in horror from the slot machine idea in which we stick in ten cent's worth of prayer, and receive ten cent's worth of unction. We utterly reject any idea that a certain

113

amount of prayer will automatically provide this. Nevertheless the Word of God does establish an intimate relationship between the two. Here is the measure of our asking and the measure of His giving: "Ye have not because ye ask not" (James 4:2). As they prayed (Acts 2:2-4), the place where they were sitting was shaken, and they were all filled with the Holy Ghost. We say that the doctrine of pentecostalism that our praying and agonising earns this greater gift of the Spirit, is a horrible thing. No! Christ, by His redemptive work, has earned the gift of the Spirit; but the gift came while the early church was praying: ". . . they were all with one accord in one place. And suddenly there came a sound from heaven . . ."

We react against the pagan idea that we can get God in a hammerlock of prayer in which, if we press hard enough, God will say 'I give in!', and then give us what we ask! We abominate that, but at the same time brethren, Christian biography and the teaching of Scripture is that, as a general rule, those who prayed most are those who knew the most unction.

The same is true with regard to the devotional reading of the Word, for it is in the assimilation of the Word as a Christian man that the truths that God has ordained for the salvation and sanctification of men become living elements of the entire inner life of the preacher: "Thy words were found and I did eat them. Thy Word was unto me the joy and rejoicing of my heart." Jeremiah, in effect, says, 'I've had it!

114

Every time I open my mouth I cause trouble. I am going to be silent. But that Word was in my heart like a fire shut up in my bones, and I was weary with forbearing, and I could not stay. If I open my mouth, I get my head chopped off! If I shut my mouth, I get spiritual heartburn! I am between the rock and the hard place; I give in to it!'

The psalmist said, "while I was musing, the fire burned." Brethren, I don't understand the interplay of all of these things! But that element of felt urgency; that element of pleading; that element of entreaty, cannot be taught. It is not something we learn in the lecture theatre, but with Paul in the closet: "Brethren, my heart's desire and prayer to God for them is that they may be saved." Such a man, when he stands before the people, cannot help but plead. He cannot help but entreat.

Let us away with all of this concept of being proper and elegant, with everything in its place! It was Alexander the Presbyterian who cried, 'O let it gush!" Oh for some holy gushing in our preaching brethren; gushing that is born of these seasons alone with God, when the realities of our faith have so impregnated the very fibres of the soul, that there cannot help but be the energy of unction in our preaching!

Bridges says:

"It is the present experience, nourishment and enjoyment that gives a glow of unction far beyond the power of academic accomplishment. It is this that causes us to bear our message written in our hearts,

115

and this is the best method to make a deep and weighty impression upon others."

Stalker, in his book in the Yale Series on preaching, speaking to this very matter, says this:

"Brethren, study God's Word diligently for your own edification; and when it has become more to you than your necessary food, sweeter than honey or the honeycomb, it will be impossible for you to speak of it to others, without a glow passing into your words which will betray the delight with which it has inspired your own heart."

Perhaps, of all causes of ministerial failure, the most common is this. Of all ministerial qualifications this, although the most simple, is the most difficult. Either we have never had a spiritual experience sufficiently deep and thorough to lay bare to us the mysteries of the soul, or our experience is too old, and we have repeated it so often that it has become stale to ourselves. Perhaps we have made reading a substitute for thinking. We may have allowed the pressures and duties of our office to curtail our prayers and to shut us out of our studies. Possibly, we have learned the professional tone in which things ought to be said, and we can fall into it without present feeling. We have learned so well what to say at the right time that we can fall into the language with no present feeling behind our words.

Seeking in Secret

Power for work like ours is only to be acquired in secret. It is only the man who has a large varied and original life with God, who can go on speaking about the things of God with fresh interest. A thousand things happen to interfere with such a prayerful and meditative life. It is not because our arguments for religion are not strong enough that we fail to convince, but because the argument is wanting in that which never fails to tell; the power of vital religion itself. People everywhere can appreciate this, and nothing can supply the lack of it. The hearers may not know why their minister, with all his gifts, does not make a religious impression upon them. It is because he himself is not a religious power.

Brethren, no one holds more firmly than I do to the fact that the Bible is the inscripturated, infallible Word of God, irrespective of whether or not anyone ever looks at it, reads it or feels its power. I have no sympathy with any kind of existential theology. No Barthian leaven operates within my thinking! But what Stalker is saying is that we can properly exegete and expound that Word, but if in so doing, there is not sensed by our people that we have a present and felt reality of the power of that Word, our preaching will be lacking in its convicting and its convincing elements. It is when the truth has become a personal conviction, that is burning in a man's heart, that he cannot be silent.

The number of truths which a man has appropriated from the Bible, and verified in his own experience, is the measure of his power. There is all the difference in the world between the man who thus speaks what he knows from an inner impulse, and the man whose sermon is simply a literary exercise on a scriptural theme, who speaks only because Sunday has come around, the bell has rung, and it is time to perform his duty. Brethren, who among us can hold his head high, in the face of such indicting words?

Balanced Ministry

The importance of our devotional exercises is to be found, not only in confirming the reality of our spiritual lives; in constantly feeding and nurturing the vitality of our spiritual lives; and in providing the soil of an anointed ministry; but fourthly, the pastor's devotional life will go far in creating the climate of a balanced ministry.

One of the tragic effects of the Fall is disharmony. Everything was in perfect equipoise in Eden. Everything Adam looked at, he interpreted properly. As surely as all his appetites were in perfect and balanced relationship, so that he never desired beyond what was legitimate, so too, his mind held all revealed truth in perfect balance. One of the fruits of the Fall is man's imbalance at the noetic level. God has given to us His Word, and the promise of a progressive sanctification, not only at the ethical and moral, but at the noetic level. When men cease to pour over the Scriptures as Christians, reading them systematically, week by week and year by year, this tendency to imbalance begins to manifest itself in a distorted view of the message of God. This in turn

118

begins to manifest itself in distorted emphases in their ministry.

There is no greater check to this tendency to imbalance than the pastor's devotional exercises. Consider 2 Tim. 3:14-17, which is directed primarily to Timothy as a man of God. The Scriptures were given to furnish him thoroughly as a man of God, that he might be furnished completely unto every good work. To do this requires systematic reading of the Scriptures as a humble disciple who comes to the feet of Jesus, saying, "Oh my great Prophet, teach me from your Word, help me to believe all that you have revealed." Such reading will deliver us from little pet theories and from avoiding hard doctrines and keep us from an imbalanced ministry.

When people ask me, "how did you become a Calvinist?", I reply "well, basically it was the systematic devotional reading of the Word that forced me into that position. I did not get it from my former schooling, but in the systematic reading through the New Testament in particular. I would come to Matthew 11, and every time I did, I would say, 'Lord there is something here that you are saying, that I don't think quite fits.' He talked about no one knowing the Son save the Father and no one knowing the Father save the Son, and revealing Him to whomsoever He wills. Then I would read in John 6: "No man can come to Me except the Father which hath sent me draw him . . ."

I had a good English teacher in the ninth grade.

He taught me the difference between 'may' and 'can.' One is a word of permission, the other a word of ability. I came to John 17. Then it was not long before I was in Romans 9, then Ephesians chapter 1. I could never let that nasty issue lie. It was there, coming out again and again. I remember the agony I would go through, saying, "Lord I want to believe and understand and receive all that you have said. What does that mean? It seems as though you are saying that in sovereign prerogative you have set your love upon some and not upon others. Lord, I confess that does not seem fair, but is that what it teaches?" Then I believed it, and would pass on to another passage in my systematic reading.

At the same time something else was happening. I noticed that Romans 9 and 10 begin with the heart throb of a passionate preacher who said, "I could wish myself accursed", and "my heart's desire and prayer is . . ." I remember saying, "Lord if I ever believe what that seems to teach, and if I come to the conviction that it is teaching what it seems to teach, then Lord help me to believe it and preach it in the way Paul believed it and preached it, holding it in a broken heart, holding it consistent with evangelistic compassion and fervour and zeal to see the lost won to yourself." Though I would not set myself up as a paragon of virtue in this, brethren, (I have tried to keep a low profile in terms of personal anecdotes), I hope the intimacy of this time warrants my saying this—I know of nothing that has been a greater check upon incipient areas of imbalance than the systematic devotional reading of the Word of God as a disciple of Jesus Christ.

Major Hindrances

What are some of the major hindrances to a pastor's devotional life? Let me deal with two categories of hindrances: the natural or the external, and then secondly, the spiritual or the internal.

Undisciplined Life

The first natural or external hindrance is an undisciplined life. God is a God of order. He made His world in an orderly way and He controls it in an orderly way. Therefore, no man functions well who does not function by order. Pastors have no clock to punch. We have no one to whom we are accountable for our hours, and we can drift into what I call the unholy art of puttering. Puttering is going about doing little inconsequential things with a lot of furore and zeal, so as to give the impression that we are very busy persons, and thus creating a little salve for our consciences. We are not really doing anything; we are just puttering, wasting time.

Scripture tells us that whatever our hand finds to do we are to do with all of our might, as unto the Lord and not unto man. M'Cheyne said that he who would increase his devotion, must increase, not his extraordinary devotions, but his ordinary devotional exercises.[3] If you are an undisciplined and

---

3. Bonar, Andrew. "Memoirs and Remains of R.M. M'Cheyne" p.54 (Banner of Truth, 1966)

unstructured man, you are going to make no progress in this area until you sit down and have a little judgment day between you and the Lord, with your calendar and clock, and work out a schedule by which to operate in the light of your God-given duties.

Unplanned Devotions

Another natural or external hindrance, in addition to an undisciplined life in general, is an unplanned devotional time in particular. The pastor simply approaches his devotional time with the attitude: 'Well what shall I do today? Shall I read a Psalm?' Or perhaps: 'I feel like an epistle today'! Brother, you must have a plan, and that plan must be governed by the peculiarities of your own body chemistry and mental furniture!

I am not one of those who can go straight from my bed up six stairs and into my study, fall on my knees, and pray. I cannot even go up and open my Bible with much profit! My mind and spirit needs to be primed by some collateral reading. In this way through the years, I have worked through many volumes, including Owen, Traill, Flavel and many other authors. Four or five pages of a good devotional author primes the pump, and gets my mind working and my spirit warmed. Recently, I have been taking a couple of columns of Gurnall's *The Christian in Complete Armour* every day for a number of months. How rich it has been!

You may not need that kind of priming. You may

be one who can go right to your Bible chapter. Find out a method that works for you. Have a plan whereby you are reading through the Scriptures systematically, not necessarily once a year, but a plan whereby you are going through the entire scope of Divine revelation, with some additional concentration on the Psalms and the Proverbs. I find that going through the Psalms continually as part of my devotional reading is very helpful, while reading the Proverbs increases my practical perspective. Find a plan and tailor it to suit your own needs.

Remaining Corruption

The greatest hindrance comes, not from these natural or external factors, but from spiritual or internal causes. The greatest one is the aversion of remaining corruption. We read in Gal. 5:17, "For the flesh lusteth against the Spirit and the Spirit against the flesh, and these are contrary the one to the other: so that ye cannot do the things that ye would." Owen makes an observation from Romans chapter 7 that has helped me tremendously in my own life. His point is that the more spiritual any activity is, the more violent will be the opposition of the flesh to that activity.

How many of you have ever said, 'well I think I will sit down, pick up the newspaper and look at the sports page,' and felt a powerful disinclination of the flesh against reading the sports page? I mean that after a busy day, you are able to sit down and read a newspaper without feeling any powerful aversion to this task. But in identical circumstances, if you pick up your Bible to read a chapter, what happens? A dullness, a lassitude comes over you like a cloud. Where does that come from? Paul replies: "When I would do good, evil is present with me" (Rom. 7:21). The more spiritual the good is, the more violent will be the opposition of remaining corruption.

It is at this point that we need to say with the apostle: "I keep under my body, and bring it into subjection . . ." (1 Cor. 9:27), or in the language of Romans 6: I have been crucified with Christ, "that the body of sin might be destroyed." Sin's chains have been broken in the Person of my Substitute. I refuse to present my members as instruments of unrighteousness to sin, but I present them as instruments of righteousness unto God.

Aversion of the Flesh

The second great spiritual or internal hindrance, the general one, is the aversion of the flesh. Brethren, let's be honest. Often we have an aversion because we have a present controversy with God. There is an area in which our consciences are not comfortable. We know that if we draw near to God, we will feel the pinch of the Spirit's pressure upon that point of controversy. Maybe you have had some angry words with your wife the night before, and you were so proud in your stinking, male, carnal, adamic pride that you did not take her into your arms and say, "Honey, forgive me. I was un-Christian; that was uncalled for." So you got up early in the morning to go to be with God and what happened? Well, there was that letter that just had to be written before the postman came—because you know that the Lord does expect us to be efficient! So you wrote that letter. Then you said, "Well, it's time to get down to pray now. Oh yes, but there is that phone call I should make . . ."! You found little things to do, in order to avoid getting down on your face before God, because you knew that the moment you did, you would have to leave that place, go downstairs and wake your wife up, and say "Honey I sinned; forgive me." Or aren't you that perverse? Brethren, any controversy with God will hinder our devotional lives.

What then, is the pathway to a fruitful devotional life? It is to recognise the indispensibility of a devotional life. It requires us to resolve to make the necessary adjustments of time and schedule to attain it. It requires us not to be discouraged when we fail. We must pick up and start again, and press on by the grace of God. May God use these thoughts from His Word, and cause us all to become more fruitful in the secret place. Then the fruits will be known by our people, as the fragrance of Christ more and more exudes from our lives and from our ministries. Amen.

Other
COVENANTER PRESS
Publications

✱ CLEFTS OF THE ROCK —Reprint

People are just starting to rediscover Macduff's 19th century works—and we are delighted to contribute this volume! Spurgeon said of his works "For an hour's pleasant and holy reading commend us to Dr Macduff," and this work is no exception. It is written in a reverent, devotional manner in which the author deals with sound theology with respect to the believer and his relationship to Christ's Person and Work—each aspect of the doctrine of Christ is set forth as a cleft in the Rock, Christ Jesus, in which a believer can hide himself for protection, comfort and strength in the Christian warfare and pilgrimage. In its practical message there is a word to the aged, bereaved and despondent, just to name three classes of Christian

In this age of superficiality and shallowness, Macduff is an exciting addition to the thankfully increasing number of titles of a sound devotional nature.

440pp Paperback $3.75

✱ CHRIST FREELY OFFERED —K. W. Stebbins

This book is a highly significant contribution to the literature available on the issue of the free offer of the Gospel. With careful exegesis and clear argument Mr Stebbins examines the biblical basis for the free offer and evaluates Reformation, Puritan, and contemporary authors on this subject.

Rev A. G. Kerr, in the Foreword, writes:

"On the one hand the writer is concerned to preserve a full

and gracious salvation, preaching Jesus Christ, freely offered
to us in the gospel, as it is expressed in the Shorter Catechism.
But on the other hand, he is concerned that this Free Offer
should be Scripturally based, solely upon our Lord's command
to go into all the world and preach the gospel. The writer
rejects the notion that we can only offer the gospel freely
if we base it upon the error of a universal love of God, or a
universal atonement."
Ken Stebbins is minister of the Presbyterian Reformed Church
at Wollongong, NSW, and lectures in Theology at John Knox
Theological College, Sydney.
128pp.Paperback $2.25

✻ WON BY BLOOD —Reprint

An exciting and challenging book for readers young and old.
Throughout the history of the Christian church there have
been faithful men and women who have hazarded their lives
for the glory of God and the salvation of sinners. 'Won by
Blood' tells of this same faithfulness.
"Through the blood of the martyrs is the seed of the church.
The intervals between sowing and harvest are sometimes long
and call for faith and patience."
This is the gripping story of the establishment of the gospel
on Erromanga—"The Martyr Isle"—Vanuatu (New Hebrides)
where a number of faithful servants of Christ gave their all
and received the Martyr's Crown.
136pp Paperback $1.35

✻ REVIVAL SET —Reprint

This is a series of paperbacks reprinted from a volume
entitled "Lectures on the Revival of Religion" first published
in 1840. The set comprises an introductory booklet "What is

True Revival", and four paperbacks—"Revival—Its Source", "Revival and the Means of Grace", "Revival—Scriptural and Historical", and "Revival in Practice".

How do we recognise true revival and how can we improve upon it; what are the hindrances to revival; when is there a need for revival and how are we to seek it? These are the questions which are raised and answered in these lectures— Important questions for today when there is such a need of a fresh outpouring of the Spirit in revival.

The authors of these lectures were godly ministers of the Church of Scotland who left the established church in 1843 and became ministers of the Free Church. These men drew upon the Scriptures, the history of the church, and their own intimate knowledge of the Work of the Holy Spirit, for they were not far removed from the glorious scenes of revival which were witnessed repeatedly in the history of the Church of Scotland up until about 1860.

In an age when there is much confusion and misunderstanding upon the subject of Revival, this reprint is timely and worthy of the attention of every believer.

4 Paperbacks, 1 Booklet, $6.00 Set.